A GUIDE TO EMPLOYMENT LAW

Oliver Rowell

Easyway Guides

Easyway Guides
61 Inniskilling
London E13 9LD   **09168726**

© Straightforward Publishing 2003

British Library Cataloguing in Publication Data. A catalogue record for this book is available from the British Library.

ISBN 1 900694 32 8

Printed by Bookcraft Wiltshire

CONTENTS

INTRODUCTION

5. Discrimination in Employment   **85**

6. Termination of Employment   **91**

7.   Unfair Dismissal   **99**

8.   Redundancy   **107**

9.   Health and Safety   **111**

Appendix 1. European legislation and UK compliance-summary

Index

INTRODUCTION

The main problem in writing a book on employment law, it seemed to me, was how to produce a slim volume, readily accessible to the beginner, at the same time embracing the whole complex legislative framework including the 2002 Employment Act which saw far reaching changes introduced into employment legislation. The Act is wide-ranging, covering work and parents, dispute resolution in the workplace, improvements to Employment Tribunal procedures, (including the introduction of an Equal pay questionnaire) provisions to implement the Fixed Term Work Directive, a right to time off for Union Learning Representatives, work focused interviews for partners of people receiving working-age benefits and some data sharing provisions. Many of the provisions of the Act are now implemented with the most recent, provisions relating to maternity/paternity pay effective from 6th April. One final provision of the Act, Work Focused Interviews, for partners of people receiving working age benefits is still under review and will not be discussed in this book.

It is hoped that this book will be a more than adequate introduction for the student or layperson, in short for all those who wish to read an informed introduction.

Throughout, there are cases, which serve to highlight main points of law. There is reference to the 1996 Employment Rights Act, which came into force on 22nd August 1996. This Act consolidated a number of existing Acts, including Employment Protection (Consolidation) Act 1978, Wages Act 1986 and Trade Union Reform and Employment Rights Act 1993.

The Disability Discrimination Act 1995 came into force in May 1996, which places greater responsibility on employers to ensure that disabled people/ employees are not disadvantaged in the sphere of employment.

Also, the Asylum and Immigration Act 1996 received royal assent on 24th July 1996, which creates the criminal offence of employing someone who does not have immigration entitlement in the U.K. The maximum penalty is a fine of up to £8,000 for each worker employed.

Industrial Tribunals (1996 ITA) were renamed Employment Tribunals on 1st August 1998 by the Employment Rights (Dispute Resolution) Act 1998. The Employment Act 2002 has introduced changes to the Tribunal procedure which will be outlined.

The Employment Relations Act 1999 covering Regulations governing maternity and parental leave becoming effective from December 15th 1999, and has been amended by the 2002 Employment Act, with provisions for parental leave and remuneration becoming effective from April 2003.

Employment law has become increasingly complex and for the person who wishes a basic introduction and who wishes to know something of their rights this book should prove invaluable.

1

Administration

Before the advent of the industrial tribunal system in 1964, labour law was regarded as an aspect of the law of contract, dealt with by the civil courts. Since 1964, the industrial tribunal system has grown and now encompasses other courts and non-judicial bodies. Industrial tribunals were renamed Employment Tribunals by the Employment Rights (Dispute Resolution) Act 1998. The Employment Tribunals Act 1996 also regulates Employment Tribunals. The 2002 Employment Act has introduced significant proposed changes to the tribunal system which are, at the time of writing, still out to consultation, expected to become law by Autumn 2003.

Most people with grievances relating to their employment will attempt to resolve these from within, utilising procedures set up by the employer. Usually, policy exists which will encompass most situations which may arise. However, in some cases, for example where unfair dismissal is alleged, Employment Tribunals are used.

Employment Tribunals

The original Industrial Tribunals were established by the Industrial Training Act 1964 to deal with certain disputes arising under the Act. They have grown in power and influence and are organised on a regional basis with each tribunal consisting of a legally qualified chairman and two lay members appointed from a panel.

Employment tribunals are empowered to deal with a wide range of matters arising from a number of legislative provisions, the most important being:

- Complaints of unfair dismissal, applications for redundancy payments,
- references regarding the written particulars of terms of employment,

- complaints regarding suspension from work on medical grounds,
- complaints regarding trade union membership and activities,
- complaints regarding the time off work provisions,
- complaints regarding the right to maternity pay and leave
- complaints under the Sex Discrimination Act 1975,
- complaints regarding time off work for anti-natal care ,
- complaints regarding secret ballots on employers premises,
- complaints regarding unreasonable expulsion from trade union membership,
- complaints from trade unions relating to failure of consultation on employment, complaints by trade unions relating to failure to consult them about transfer of undertakings.

Employment Tribunal Reform-The 2002 Employment Act

Part 2 of the 2002 Employment Act concerns Employment Tribunal Procedure. It covers changes to the costs regime, amendments to ACAS powers and new rules in relation to practice directions and pre-hearing reviews.

Costs awards against representatives personally

Section 22 of the 2002 EA deals with costs awards against representatives because of their conduct-the twist in the tale being that representatives cannot pass costs on to clients. Representatives will, however, be able to appeal against any personal costs order made. It is unlikely that any costs award, which includes the personal element for the representative, will exceed the current statutory maximum costs award of £10,000.

Costs-preparation time

Tribunals are to be authorized to order that one party pick up the bill for the others preparation costs. Parties will be able to claim the costs of preparation time or legal fees but not both.

Conciliation-new 'fixed period' for ACAS

ACAS currently has a duty to promote settlement in a wide range of employment rights disputes and provides its services literally up to the doors of the Employment Tribunal. S24 of the 2002 EA proposes changes to avoid the large number of last minute settlements. ACAS will be given a fixed period in order to conciliate to settle the case. The case itself will effectively be stayed and no hearing date set. Once the fixed period is complete, the case will go forward for hearing.

Power to delegate prescription of forms

S25 of the 2002 EA will give the secretary of State powers to prescribe the forms that must be used to commence and defend Employment Tribunal claims. At present there are no set forms-only certain key pieces of information, which must be provided.

Practice directions

Currently, the President of the Employment Tribunals does not have power to issue practice directions, which ensure uniformity of procedure amongst tribunals. This has now changed under the Act and the President has been given the requisite powers.

Pre-hearing reviews

Pre-hearing reviews can be an effective way of dispensing with weak cases early in the course of proceedings. The Act seeks to strengthen the tribunal's powers to weed out weak cases, by making it clear that cases can be struck out at a PHR-but only where the ordering of a deposit would not be sufficient.

The procedure in Employment Tribunals is regulated by the Employment Rights Act 1996, as amended by the Employment Act 2002.. Rules provide for pre-hearing of assessments of Employment Tribunal cases at which the tribunal may warn either party to the proceedings that if he wishes to continue an order of costs may be made against him if he loses. The proceedings are intended to be relatively informal both in terms of the pre-tribunal procedure and the hearing. The reasons for the decision of a tribunal must be recorded in a document signed by the chairperson and he must state in this document whether the reasons are recorded in a full or summary form. Full reasons must be recorded in certain types of cases, for example, under the Equal Pay Act, Sex Discrimination Act or the Race Relations Act.

Breach of contract claims will be heard by the Chair of the Tribunal alone, unless the chair considers that the matter should be heard by a full Tribunal. By s 4(3) of the Employment Tribunals Act 1996, in addition to breach of contract claims, the Chair of a Tribunal can hear certain other claims alone. These include the right not to suffer unauthorised or excessive deductions in respect of trade union subscriptions, the employers failure to pay remuneration under a protective award, the right to receive written particulars, a statement of changes to the particulars or an itemised pay statement, the right to guarantee payments, the right of remuneration for suspension on medical grounds, the right to a redundancy payment, an application for an employers payment against the Secretary of State for Employment, the appointment of an authorised person to conduct certain proceedings under the ERA 1996 where an employee has died and has no personal representative and a failure to pay compensation for failing to inform or consult over a transfer of undertaking.

In addition, the chairperson alone may hear any claim, if the parties agree in writing. The 1998 Act also provides that the Tribunal may dispense with an oral hearing where the parties have given their written consent, and may determine a case hearing only evidence from an applicant where the party against whom proceedings are brought has not contested the case or, where the applicant is not seeking relief the Tribunal has the power to grant the applicant such relief.

Appeals on questions of law lie in respect of most of the jurisdictions of the Employment tribunals to the Employment Appeal Tribunal, regulated by the Employment Tribunals Act. In respect of most of the kinds of application, which may be made to the Employment tribunals, before there is a hearing, an attempt is made to settle the matter by conciliation using the services of a conciliation officer.

Employment Appeal Tribunal (EAT)

The EAT was established in 1975. The legislation governing the EAT is now the Employment Tribunals Act 1996. It consists of judges of the High Court and Court of Appeal one of whom is appointed president, and lay members drawn from a panel of persons having special knowledge of industrial relations.

The essential function of the EAT is to hear appeals on questions of law from the Employment tribunals on most of the jurisdictions exercised by the tribunals and to hear appeals (some on questions of law only and others on questions of law and fact) from the Certification Officer. The EAT has only limited jurisdiction allowing it to determine some applications for compensation following the refusal of a trade union to admit or re-admit a person to membership of a closed shop.

The EAT regulates its own procedure subject to the provisions of the ETA 1996. A party who wishes to appeal an industrial tribunal's decision must submit a copy of the full written reason for the decision in addition to a notice of appeal and a copy of the decision within 42 days.

The EAT does, however, have a discretion to authorise the institution of the appeal before the full written reasons are sent if it considers it would lead to more "expeditious or economic disposal of any proceedings or would otherwise be desirable in the interests of justice". An appeal from the EAT on a question of law lies to the Court of Appeal and thence from the House of Lords.

Advisory Conciliation and Arbitration Service (ACAS)

ACAS was established in 1974. It is independent of Government and is managed by a council normally consisting of a full time chairman and nine other members, including three appointed after consultation with the representatives of employers organisations and three appointed after consultation with workers representatives. ACAS is based in London with offices based in regional centres. ACAS has the power to appoint staff, including conciliation officers, and to request other persons to perform services, e.g., arbitration.

Codes of Practice

The publication and use of codes of practice by ACAS is becoming of increasing importance in the regulation of employment and industrial relations. The status in law of codes is that, although a failure to observe any provision of a code cannot of itself give rise to legal proceedings, in proceedings before industrial tribunals and other bodies the provisions of a code are admissible in evidence and are to be taken into account in determining the question at issue.

In Polkey v. A.E. Dayton Services Ltd (1987) the House of Lords reaffirmed the importance of the appropriate codes in determining the fairness of dismissal.

ACAS has issued the following codes:

Disciplinary practice and procedures in employment

Disclosures of information to trade unions for collective bargaining purposes

Time off for trade union duties and activities.

Central Arbitration Committee (CAC)

The CAC was established in 1975 by the Employment Protection Act (now s259 of the 1992 Act) and replaced the Industrial Arbitration Board. Although independent of government and ACAS, CAC is served by ACAS staff. CAC has a chairman and members appointed by the Secretary of State for Employment.

The main function of CAC is hearing complaints following an employer's failure to disclose information for collective bargaining purposes. There is no appeal from CAC but it is subject to judicial review if it exceeds its jurisdiction or powers.

Certification Officer

The office of CO was created in 1975 (EPA 1975 s7) The main functions of the CO are to determine whether a trade union is entitled to a certificate of independence, to maintain a list of trade unions and employers associations and to perform certain duties under the Trade Union Act 1913 (amended) in relation to the political fund of the trade unions.

The Employment Act 1988 added two further powers in this respect. Section 16 created the right to complain to the CO (or the High Court) where a trade union member claims a political fund ballot has been or will be held otherwise than in accordance with the rules drawn up by the CO. S22 allows the CO to regulate his own procedure, including a power to 'restrict the circumstances in which the identity of an individual who has made, or is proposing to make, any such application, or complaint is disclosed to any person. The purpose of this is to prevent a complainant from being victimised. The 1992 Trade Union and Labour Relations Act now governs (s2 and 123). Any appeals from decisions of the CO are heard by the Employment Appeal Tribunal.

Commissioner for the Rights of Trade Union Members

The Employment Act 1988 s 19 (now s266 of the 1992 Trade Unions and Labour Relations Act) empowers the Secretary of State for Employment to appoint a commissioner for the Rights of Trade Union Members in relation to the following:

-a failure to hold a proper ballot before industrial action, the right to inspect a trade unions accounts and records, the recovery of union funds used to indemnify unlawful conduct, the restraint of trustees from acting unlawfully, a failure to comply with the CO's rules for conducting a political fund ballot, failure to comply with the provisions of the Trade Union Act regulating election to a unions principal executive council, the misuse of union funds for unapproved political purposes, such other matters as may be specified in an order made by the Secretary of State for Employment.

The areas where the commissioner may offer assistance have been extended by the Employment Act 1990 and the trade union Reform and Employment Rights Act 1993 and include failure to comply with balloting provisions in respect of industrial action or the election of officers or the political fund and other areas. Clause 25 of the Employment Relations Act 1999 abolishes the above post and transfers the powers to the certification officer.

The Secretary of State for Employment

The main functions of the above are:

- Approving agreements making provision for payments to redundant persons

- Approving Codes of Practice and seeking Parliamentary approval for them

- Approving dismissals procedure agreements

- Receiving notification of proposed redundancies

- Approving guarantee payments agreements

- Reviewing various financial limits

- Making regulations upon a wide range of matters

In addition, the Secretary of State for Employment has responsibility for issuing, after consultation with ACAS, Codes of Practice containing such practical guidance as he thinks fit for the purpose of promoting the improvement of industrial relations and keeping such codes of practice under review. As with codes issued by ACAS, a failure to observe the provisions of such a code of practice does not of itself render a person liable to proceedings, but in any proceedings before a court, industrial tribunal or the CAC, a Code is admissible in evidence. To date, the Secretary of State has issued three codes of practice on picketing (limiting number of pickets),closed shop agreements and Draft codes for Industrial Action Ballots.

Powers of the courts

The most important matters with which the courts are concerned are actions by employees for damages following injury at work, actions in tort arising from industrial action, actions for breach of contract including breach of a covenant in restraint of trade and prosecutions under the health and safety legislation.

European Court of Justice

Because it belongs to the European Community, Britain is bound by the decisions of the European Court of Justice. The decisions are only relevant where there is a conflict between British and European law. An industrial tribunal, employment appeals tribunal or any court may (by virtue of article 177 of the Treaty of Rome) refer a case to the ECJ where there is a question of any conflict between the two sets of law. On of the major sources of reference to the ECJ has been the law on equal pay. However, in Pickstones v. Freemans PLC (1988) the Court of Appeal felt able to apply European Law directly without reference to the ECJ. In light of this decision, it can be argued that European law is being incorporated directly into English law without having passed through any parliamentary process.

The Equal Opportunities Commission

The EOC was established by the Sex Discrimination Act 1975s 53. It consists of between eight and fifteen commissioners in addition to its full time staff. The three general duties of the EOC are to work towards the elimination of discrimination in employment and elsewhere, to promote equality of opportunity between men and women and to keep under review the Equal Pay Act 1970 and the Sex Discrimination Act 1975. The EOC produces an annual report for presentation to Parliament and is also empowered to produce Codes of Practice.

The main powers of the EOC in relation to employment are to carry out investigations, in the course of which if it is satisfied that a breach of the Sex Discrimination Act or Equal Pay Act has occurred, it may issue a non discrimination notice against which there is a right of appeal to an industrial tribunal. The effect of a non discrimination notice which is kept on a register is that in the following five years the EOC may apply to a county court if it considers that a further breach of the legislation is likely. Further powers are to bring proceedings in respect of discriminatory advertising or instruction or pressure to discriminate and to give assistance to aggrieved persons.

Commission for Racial Equality

The CRE was established by s 43 of the Race Relations Act 1976. It's functions in relation to Racial discrimination are similar to the EOC in relation to discrimination dealt with by the Sex Discrimination Act.

The Health and Safety Commission

The Health and Safety Commission was established by the Health and Safety at work Act 1974. The HSC is responsible to the Secretary of State and has a number of duties, the main ones being to assist and encourage persons to further the general provisions of the 1974 Act, to make arrangements for research and the promotion of training and information connected with it, to act as an information advisory service, to submit proposals for regulations and to approve and issue codes of practice.

Health and Safety Executive

The HSE was established by s10 of the Health and Safety at Work Act 1974. The HSE is answerable to the Health and Safety Commission except as regards the enforcement of the health and safety at work legislation. The function of the HSE is to enforce the health and safety at work legislation by means of inspection of premises, the issuing of improvement and prohibition notices, prosecution etc.

Commissioner for Protection against Unlawful Industrial Action

This is a post created by the 1993 Trade Union Reform and Employment Rights Act by inserting a new section into the 1992 Trade Union Act. The Commissioner has the power to assist any party who wishes to take proceedings on the basis that the supply of goods and services to him as an individual has been prevented or delayed by unlawful industrial action or that quality of goods and services has been affected (s235A). Such assistance may be in the form of bearing of legal costs and/or representation, and in the form of an indemnity in respect of costs or liability incurred.

Dispute resolution generally-changes introduced in the 2002 Employment Act

The Employment Act 2002 has introduced statutory disciplinary and grievance procedures into employment contracts. Section 3 of the Act, dealing with this are, makes substantial changes to unfair dismissal legislation.

The governments aim is to encourage employees and employers to conciliate their disputes in the workplace, rather than resorting to Employment Tribunals. In particular, the government is concerned by the number of disputes involving small businesses which constitute

21

nearly one third of all Tribunal cases. These small businesses often have no or inadequate procedures for dealing with or resolving employee disputes. At the time of writing these provisions are about to be implemented. ACAS can provide the necessary information concerning implementation dates. It is expected that late 2003 wil see the changes introduced.

New Statutory Dispute Resolution Procedures

The Act introduces two new statutory dispute resolution procedures:

- Dismissal and disciplinary procedures
- Grievance procedure

These will form part of an individuals contract of employment (see next chapter) and must either be set out in the contract itself or be readily available in a document, which is referred to in the contract. They will provide a minimum level of procedure, which must be followed by employers and employees when dealing with disputes.

Any agreement to contract out of these new statutory procedures will be unlawful. Failure to follow these procedures will not only have the consequences set out below, but will also separately amount to a breach of contract.

Dismissal and disciplinary procedures

There are two DDP procedures contained in schedule 2 of the Act-a standard procedure and a modified (shorter) procedure. Whilst the detail will be fleshed out in Regulations, it is expected that the standard procedure will be mandatory, in the majority of disciplinary issues, with the modified procedure only being available for extremely severe cases of gross misconduct. The main features of the standard procedure are:
- Step 1-the employer must set out in writing the employee's alleged misconduct and invite the employee to discuss the matter
- Step 2-the employer must convene a meeting. The employee must

take all reasonable steps to attend the meeting. At the end of the meeting, the employer must notify the employee of his decision and his right of appeal

- Step 3-If the employee exercises his right of appeal, the employer must convene an appeal hearing. The employee must take all reasonable steps to attend. At the end of the appeal hearing, the employer must notify the employee of his decision.

Unfair dismissal and the statutory DDPs

If an employer fails to follow a DDP, in circumstances where he is required to use one, an employee's dismissal will be automatically unfair. As with normal unfair dismissal claims, this will only apply to employees with at least one year's service.

Compensation for failure to follow DDP

If the failure is due to the employer, the tribunal must increase the compensatory element of their award by 10%. Only where it would be unjust or inequitable can the tribunal decide not to make an adjustment or to make a lesser adjustment. It will also have the discretion to increase the award up to a maximum of 50%. If the failure to follow the DDP was down to the employee then the tribunal has the power to reduce the award.

Failure to follow a non-DDP procedure

The 2002 Employment Act has amended the Employment Rights Act 1998 by introducing a new section 98A. Providing an employer has complied with the DDP requirements of the disciplinary procedure, failure to comply with, or follow the provisions of its procedure, which are over and above the DDP, will not render a dismissal unfair, if the employer can show that even if the full disciplinary procedure had been followed, he would nevertheless have dismissed the employee.

Grievance procedures

There are two new statutory grievance procedures-a standard one and a shorter modified procedure. The main features are as follows:

- Step 1-the employee must set out his grievance in writing and send this to the employer.
- Step 2-the employer must convene a meeting and the employee must take all reasonable steps to attend the meeting. After the meeting, the employer must inform the employee of his decision and notify the employee of his right to appeal.
- Step 3-If the employee wishes to appeal, the employer must convene an appeal hearing. The employee must take all reasonable steps to attend. After the meeting the employer must inform the employee of his decision.

Regulations will provide full details as to when the GP will apply, although schedule 4 of the 2002 EA already sets out the jurisdictions where the GP will operate. This covers the majority of employment complaints including:

- Unfair dismissal
- Sex, race or disability discrimination
- Unlawful deduction from wages
- National minimum wage
- Working time
- Equal pay
- Redundancy

Prohibition on Tribunal claims where the GP has not been followed

S.32 of the 2002 EA introduces a radical concept. An employee wil be prevented from actually presenting a claim at the employment tribunal if the subject mater of the claim was one where he should have used the GP and has either failed to do so, or has failed to allow the employer at least 28 days in which to respond to the grievance. The purpose behind this provision is clear-to require employees and employers to at least attempt to resolve their problems before seeking recourse to the Employment Tribunal.

Compensation levels will be affected where there has been a failure to follow a GP. As with the DDP, compensation payments will either be reduced or increased if there has been a failure to follow a GP.

Time limits for presenting cases to the Employment Tribunal

The Act states that regulations can be made to increase the time period for the presentation of claims where the DDP or GP applies. It is likely that this will mean that employees will have longer than the usual three months in which to bring their claim if the DDP or GP have been used and the requisite procedures have not been completed within the existing time limits.

2

Contracts of Employment

A contract of employment will use the terms 'employee' or 'servant' which distinguishes it from a contract of services under which an independent contractor performs services under contract for another person. Legally, the contractor is self-employed and the distinction between an employee and independent contractor is significant. Many Acts of Parliament and statutory regulations demand such a distinction. For example, part V1 of the Employment Protection (consolidation) Act 1978 (now 1996 Employment Rights Act) extends only to persons who are employees. Furthermore, the system of taxation is different as between self-employed and employed persons.

In addition, the concept of vicarious liability normally extends only to the employer/employee relationship. Vicarious liability means that an employer is responsible for the legal consequences of act done by his employees during the course of work. There are also certain implied terms, such as rights duties and obligations which are implied into every contract of employment, but they do not extend to self employed.

The question of whether the relationship of employer/employee exists is a matter for determination by the courts rather than relying solely on the description or label attached to the contract by the parties. Young and Woods v. West (1980): the Court of Appeal stated that whether a person is to be regarded as self-employed or employed is a question of law not fact. The label which the parties attach to the relationship may be relevant to determining that relationship but it is not conclusive. The courts have developed several tests for distinguishing between employees and independent contractors.

The tests are as follows:

a. The control test. Does the person alleged to be the employer actually control the employee in respect of the work done and the performance of that work. If the answer was in the affirmative the relationship of employer/employee was established.

b. The integration test. This test was first stated in precise terms by Denning LJ in Stevenson, Jordan and Harrison v. Macdonald and Evans (1952):

'One feature which seems to run through the instances is that, under a contract of service, a man is employed as part of the business, and his work is done as an integral part of the business: whereas, under a contract for services, his work, although done for the business, is not integrated into it, but is only accessory to it'

c. The economic reality test. In recent years the courts have used a more flexible approach which incorporates both of the previous tests. This is referred to as the economic reality test and means that factors such as control, integration and powers of selection etc are simply issues which contribute to the decision which must be based on all the circumstances.

One important case was Ready Mixed Concrete (South East) Limited v Pensions and National Insurance (1968). The worker to whom the case related was the driver of a lorry, which he obtained on hire purchase from the company. He was required to paint the lorry in the companies colours and had to obey instructions from the company's servants. On the other hand, he could use substitute drivers if he was ill or on holiday and the contract stated that he was not to be regarded as an employee. In other words, certain terms of the contract tended to suggest that he was employed whilst others pointed to him being self-employed. The question arose as to whether he was an employee. Held: there are three conditions which establish a contract of service:

a. The employee agrees to provide his own work and skill
b. There must be some element of control exercisable by the employer: and-

c. The other terms of the contract must not be inconsistent with a contract of service.

In this case, a consideration of point (c) and particularly the question of the use of substitute drivers led to the finding that the driver was an independent contractor.

Recently, the tribunals and courts have tended to ask the single fundamental question: 'is the person who has engaged himself to perform these services performing them as a person in business on his own account'. Young and Woods V West (1980) is an important case in this respect. West worked for the appellants as a sheet metal worker, however, choosing to pay his own tax and National Insurance. He had no entitlement to holiday or sick pay. Following the termination of his contract he claimed to be an employee and pursued a claim for unfair dismissal. The Court of Appeal, applying the above test, said that it was impossible to regard West as being in business on his own account. Apart from handling his own deductions, and having no holiday or sick pay, Wests conditions were the same as other workers.

One of the many problems arising out of the distinction between an employee and an independent contractor is that, particularly in the construction industry, workers are often taken on the basis that they are self-employed, although, to all intents and purposes, they may appear employed. This is called the "lump" which means that the person contracting his services is paid a lump sum payment and takes care of his own tax, national insurance etc. The employer is absolved of responsibility for PAYE etc. Since 1971, legislative provisions have existed whose purpose is to minimise the income tax evasion through use of a system of exempting certificates available only to genuine sub-contractors. The most recent of these provisions are those contained in the finance Act 1979.

Form of contract

With two exceptions (merchant seamen and apprentices) there is no requirement that the contract of employment be in writing. However, this can lead to difficulties of providing proof and the contracts of Employment Act 1963 was passed (subsequently the 1972 Act) with the objective of ensuring that most employees were provided with some written evidence of the main terms of employment. These provisions were contained in part 1 of the Employment Protection Act 1978, now consolidated into the 1996 ERA which applies to all employees except registered dock workers, workers working wholly or mainly outside Great Britain, part time employees who do not have continuity of employment and Crown employees.

Section 1 of the 1978 Act states that employers to whom the Act relates must provide employees with a written statement laying out the following particulars: Names of parties and date of commencement and the date on which the employee's period of continuous service began:

The scale or rate of Remuneration or the method of calculating it;
How often paid:
Hours of work:
Holidays and holiday pay:
Terms and conditions relating to sickness:
Pensions:
Length of notices entitlement when terminating contract, or, where the contract is for a fixed term, date of expiry of contract:
Title of job:
Disciplinary rules:
Grievance procedures:
Whether a contracting-out certificate is in force relating to that employment.

Although there is a requirement to include a note in the written particulars specifying disciplinary rules applicable to the employee if the employer has more than 20 employees, as we have seen in the previous chapter, the 2002 Employment Act has introduced the necessity to include in all contracts a Statutory Disciplinary and Grievance procedure. This has been fully explained above.

The written statement is not a contract but is merely evidence of certain terms of the contract of employment. Nor are the statement of terms finally conclusive.

Vicarious liability

The basic principle of vicarious liability is that the employer is liable for the torts (negligence) of employees whilst employed by him (during the course of employment). The key here is 'during the course of employment'. As Lord Porter said in Weaver v. Tredegar Iron and Coal Company Ltd (1940):

'The man's work does not consist solely in the task which he is employed to perform, it also included matters incidental to that task. Times during which meals are taken, moments during which the man is proceeding to his work from one portion of his employers premises to another and periods of rest may all be included. Nor is his work necessarily confined to his employer's premises'

Vicarious criminal liability

As a general rule an employer is not liable for the criminal offences committed by his employees during the course of employment. However, in modern times a number of statutory exceptions have been created to this rule, particularly as regards offences committed by the employees of corporate bodies, e.g., under the Trade Descriptions Act 1968 and the Health and Safety at Work Act etc 1974.

Selection of employees

A number of statutory restrictions have been introduced which affect the employer's right to employ who he chooses. The main ones are the Disability Discrimination Act 1996: the Rehabilitation of Offenders Act 1974, the Sex Discrimination Act 1975 and the Race Relations Act 1976.

Rehabilitation of Offenders Act 1974

The 1974 Act allows a person to 'live down' certain convictions after a specified period of between six months and ten years, depending on the conviction and sentence, a conviction is deemed to be spent providing no serious offence has been committed during the rehabilitation period.

The Act provides that normally a spent conviction or failure to disclose it, is no ground for refusing to employ or dismiss a person or discriminate against him in employment. It should be noted that regulations under the Act means that it does not apply to a number of kinds of employment including teaching, medicine, accountancy etc.

Continuous employment

The concept of 'continuous employment is very important in that nearly all of the various statutory rights afforded employees are dependent upon the acquisition by the employee of two years continuous employment, as a minimum. The rules for computing the period of continuous employment are contained in schedule 13 of the 1996 Employment Rights (Consolidation) Act.

Employment is presumed to be continuous unless the contrary is shown. Any week in which the employee is employed for sixteen hours or more counts towards computing the period of employment. These do not include 'hours on call'. Sickness injury etc does not discount weeks.

One vital question is: can separate concurrent contracts, with the same employer, be aggregated in order to give a person continuity of employment? In Lewis v. Surrey County Council (1987) L had worked for the council since 1969 in three art colleges. L had separate contract for each college term and for each of the three courses. Each contract was confined to the particular department concerned. The contract merely specified the total number of hours to be worked. The House of Lords held that the contracts could not be aggregated as the legislation referred to only one single contractual obligation. The House of Lords did however indicate that L should have pleaded that the three contracts amounted to one single contract.

Any week in which an employee is absent on account of a 'temporary cessation' of work counts in the calculation of a period of continuous employment. Any week during which an employee is absent counts towards continuous employment if, by arrangement or custom, the employment is regarded as continuous. Any week in which an employee is on strike, or absent from work because of a lock out, does not count in computing the period of employment but does not break continuity. If an employee is employed for more than 16 hours per week and then becomes employed for less than 16 hours but more than 8 hours, he will, for a further period of twenty-six weeks, be treated as employed for more than 16 hours per week. If an employee has been employed for more than 8 hours per week, but less than 16, and has been so employed for five years, he is regarded as being continuously employed for that period.

Transfer of undertakings

There are various provisions dealing with the question of continuity of employment for the purposes of employment protection rights. The 1978 Act Schedule 13 and the Transfer of Undertakings (protection of Employment) Regulations 1981 deal with these. The net effect of the provisions is that where there is a transfer to a new employer, continuity is not broken.

SPECIFIC EMPLOYMENT CONTRACTS

Some groups of employees are in a special position with regard to contracts of employment.

Directors and partners

A company director is regarded as an employee for most of the statutory purposes if he has a written service contract with the company, but a non-executive director is not usually regarded as an employee. Whether such a service contract exists is a matter of law, to be determined by reference to the facts of the particular case. Thus, even the director of a one-man business may be an employee.

One important case dealing with the employment rights of directors is that of Eaton v. Robert Eaton and Secretary of State for Employment (1988). Eaton was the managing director of RE Ltd. When the company ceased trading, he applied to the tribunal for a redundancy payment. No payment was granted as there was nothing in writing to indicate that E was an employee of the company and since 1981 E had not received any financial Remuneration from the company because of its financial position. The EAT supported the decision of the tribunal as they could not find fault with the finding that E was an 'office holder' and therefore not an employee.

Partners

A partner in a firm is self-employed. If a person is employed by partners, the relationship of employer/employee exists.

Apprentices

A contract of apprenticeship is an agreement whereby the apprentice binds himself to the employer to learn the trade. Such a contract must be in writing: Apprentices Act 1814. The contract may only be terminated by the employer if the apprentice clearly demonstrates an intention not to learn or for gross misconduct. Conversely, the apprentice may only terminate the contract if the employer fails to provide instruction. Although apprentices are entitled to claim statutory rights of unfair dismissal and/or redundancy, the expiry of an apprenticeship contract is not of itself unfair dismissal or redundancy.

Public sector employees

In the case of Crown servants, a relationship is enjoyed between Crown and employee which is analogous to a contract of employment, subject to an implied right of the Crown to dismiss without notice. Employees of nationalised industries and local authorities are not Crown employees. Unless an Act so provides, it does not bind the Crown. A number of modern employment law provisions, however, have been extended to cover the Crown.

Police

The police are excluded from many of the statutory rights to which other employees are entitled, e.g. the right to present a complaint of unfair dismissal. The definition of police service in the 1978 Act is wide enough to include police officers. One important case was Home Office v. Robinson and the Prison Officers Association (1981). In addition, the rights of police officers to be members of trade unions and to engage in industrial action are severely limited. However, as 'office holders' police officers cannot be dismissed without a hearing and have a right to reinstatement in the event of the dismissal being found to be wrongful.

The armed forces

The armed forces are excluded from the various statutory rights enjoyed by employees. One of the questions which has been recently raised is whether or not a public sector employee is able to have the decision of his/her dismissal reviewed by the court through the judicial review procedure. As the normal route of Industrial Tribunal cannot be followed by an 'office holder' e.g. a police officer, judicial review is appropriate to obtain a remedy as there is no alternative. The mere existence of a contract however, will not stop a court from reviewing a decision where it thinks appropriate. One important case is McGoldrick v. London Borough of Brent (1987).

Minors

The ordinary rule of the law of contract is to the effect that a minor (person under eighteen) is bound by a contract of employment if the agreement as a whole is substantially to that persons benefit. In Doyle v. White City Stadium LTD and the British Boxing Board of Control (1935) an infant boxer held a BBBC license to box. After one contest he was disqualified and in accordance with BBBC rules his purse withheld. He claimed that the contract was not binding on him so the purse could not be withheld. The courts held that the contract was substantially to his benefit so the BBBC was within its rights to withhold the purse.

In addition to common law there are some statutory restrictions covering minors. The Children and Young Persons Act of 1933 and the Employment of Children Act 1973 regulate the employment of those minors below school leaving age (16). These Acts prevent the employment of any person under 13. Between the ages of 13-16 a minor may be employed in part time work subject to the restrictions as to the number of hours which may be worked and as to the time of such work. In addition, there are restrictions as to the employment in certain jobs, e.g. factories and mines. Between the ages of 16 and 18, minors are classed as young persons and in various legislative provisions restrictions are imposed upon the kind of work and the number of hours which such persons may do.

The Sex Discrimination Act 1986 removes most of the existing statutory provisions restricting women's hours of work. Clauses 4-7 of the Employment Bill 1988 (now 1996 ERA) seeks to modify the differences between working conditions for women. Clause 8 seeks to repeal the majority of decisions relating to employment of 'young persons'. The aims of these repeals is to remove restrictions on hours and holidays.

Temporary employees

Once an employee has completed the appropriate period for continuous employment (notably two years for unfair dismissal) he is eligible to claim the various statutory rights. An employee who is engaged expressly as a temporary employee to replace someone suspended on medical grounds or absent on maternity leave is not normally regarded as unfairly dismissed when the absent employee returns.

Probationary employees

An employee may be engaged subject to a probationary period, the employer retaining the right to terminate or confirm the contract within or at the end of the specified time. Once the employee has completed the stated time he is eligible to present a complaint of unfair dismissal. As with any other dismissal, which is alleged to be unfair, the employer must show that he acted reasonably. Regular appraisals are seen as necessary evidence by tribunals in order to demonstrate that the employee under probation knew he may be dismissed.

Employees on fixed term-contracts

Under such contracts employment rights depend whether the contracts can be aggregated in order to give the employee continuous employment. There is no statutory definition of fixed term contract. However, following the decision in BBC v. Dixon (1979) it is clear that a fixed term contract is not fixed if it contains a clause for early termination. A fixed term contact is one which expires on a particular date, rather than on the performance of a task or the happening of an event.

Fixed-Term Working regulations

The 2002 Employment Act implement the long-awaited Fixed Term Employees (Prevention of less Favourable Treatment) Regulations which will finally came into force on 1st October 2002. In summary, the following will be covered:

- Fixed term workers cannot be treated less favourably than their colleagues who are permanent employees unless there is an objective reason for doing so.
- Fixed term workers can compare themselves with colleagues who are engaged by the same employer who do the same or broadly similar work.
- The use of successive fixed-term contracts will be limited to four

years unless the use of further fixed-term contracts is justified on objective grounds.

- From 1st October 2002 redundancy waivers will not be valid.
- Rights under these regulations will be enforced in the Employment Tribunals.

Government training schemes

The status of persons on these schemes depends on its nature. For example, Youth Training Schemes are aimed primarily at training as its objects are those of work experience and learning. Therefore a person on such a scheme is not an employee.

Clearly, if a person is an employee under the scheme then service with an employer will count towards continuous employment. However, in schemes where the person is not an employee, previous training will not count towards continuity.

Persons over retiring age

The law in this area has recently been changed because of the European Court of Justice decision in Marshall v. Southampton and South West Hampshire Area Health Authority. (1986) This decision meant that the equal treatment directive was directly applicable to state employees, but legislation was required to provide a remedy for private sector employees. The decision concerned men and women being required to retire at different ages which the ECJ held to be discriminatory. The response of the Government was to pass the Sex Discrimination Act 1986 which gave effect to the decision in Marshall but also made other amendments.

TERMS OF CONTRACT

Significance of the terms of contract

In any dispute between an employer and employee, the terms of the contract are of considerable significance in that one party may have a right to take legal action against the other in respect of any breach of contract. Of more importance is the significance of the terms of contract when an action for unfair dismissal is brought. In such a case, although the question of whether one or more parties has broken the contract is of considerable importance, other considerations arise-notably whether the employer acted reasonably in dismissing the employee.

Prior to the introduction of the remedy of unfair dismissal, an employer could always terminate the contract provided that he gave proper notice. The employee would have no recourse in law.

Sources of the terms of the contract

The terms of the contract of employment may be derived from a number of sources: minimum statutory standards; express statements of the parties; collective agreements; works rules books; custom; duties of employees; duties of employers.

It should be noted that, by virtue of the 1996 Employment Rights Act, an employer is under an obligation to supply his employees with a written statement containing information as to certain terms of the contract of employment.

Minimum Statutory Standards

In effect all those statutory rights and duties which apply to the employer/employee relationship may be said to form part of every contract of employment except those to which the statutory provisions do not apply. With very few exceptions it is not possible for parties to contract out of statutory provisions.

Minimum terms orders

Certain bodies, notably wage councils, are empowered to make orders which take effect as part of individual contracts of employment and are enforceable as such. It should be noted that the powers of wage councils were limited by the Wages Act 1986, itself consolidated by the 1996 Employment Rights Act.

Express statements of the parties

Nature of express statements. An express statement, in this context, is a statement, either oral or written, made by the employer to the employee (or vice versa) concerning the terms of the contract. Such statements may include letters of appointment, formal contracts drawn up by the employer, verbal statements as to the terms and conditions of employment upon which the person is to be employed (as to wages hours holidays etc) or other statements.

If an express statement is made before the parties enter into the contract of employment, it forms part of the contract and may not be subsequently altered without the mutual consent of the parties. If one party deviates from the agreed pre-contractual terms, that party is in breach of contract unless the other consents to the deviation either expressly or by deviation.

Post-contractual statements. Post contractual statements do not form part of the contract of employment unless the parties expressly or implicitly agree that such a statement does become part of the contract. If an employee is employed upon certain terms which are not stated prior to the commencement of the contract and he is subsequently given a written statement which differs from the original terms the written statement does not supersede the written terms because the written statement is not to be regarded as contractual but merely as evidence of the contract.

Collective agreements

The term 'collective agreement' has a particular definition in s 178 (1) of the Trade Unions and Labour Relations (consolidation) Act 1992. However, in general terms it may be described as an agreement between a trade union and an employer or employers association which deals, amongst other things, with the terms and conditions of employment of employees of the employer who is a party to the agreement. A collective agreement must be considered at two levels:

a) its effect as between the parties to it;

b) Its effect upon the individual contract of employment of the employees who are the object of the agreement.

It has been estimated that 75% of all employees have their terms and conditions of employment determined by collective agreements and it is therefore important to know the extent to which as a matter of law, such agreements form part of the individual contract of employment. This is sometimes referred to as the 'normative' effect of collective agreements. Several arguments have been advanced to suggest that a collective agreement must automatically be regarded as forming part of the contracts of employment of those employees to whom the agreement refers; but these arguments have generally been refuted by the courts.

The correctness of this view has been put under pressure by the Court of Appeal decision in Marley v Forward Trust Group Ltd (1986). M was employed as a field supervisor in F's Bristol office. His terms and conditions of employment incorporated the terms of a collective agreement with ASTMS, and included both a mobility and redundancy clause, the latter allowing a six-month trial period. However, the final clause of the agreement stated that the agreement is binding in honour only.

F closed their Bristol office and M worked in London, under the terms of the agreement, for a trial period. He found the job unsuitable and sought a redundancy payment. Both the IT and the EAT rejected his claim on the ground that the agreement was stated to be binding in honour only and was, accordingly, unenforceable. The Court of Appeal rejected this and held that the terms of an unenforceable collective agreement can be incorporated into contracts of employment and are then enforceable against the individual employee. The unenforceable nature of the agreement was limited to the parties to the agreement, in this case the employer and the union.

Express incorporation. It is fairly well established that it is possible to incorporate a collective agreement into an individual contract of employment if the contract expressly provides that this is to be the case. In National Coal Board v Galley (1958) it was held that a clause of a collective agreement which stated that colliery deputies would work 'such days or part days in each week as may reasonably be required by the employer' could be regarded as being part of the original contracts of employment, because the contracts of the deputies referred to that collective agreement as being the source of the terms of the contracts.

It should be noted that the written statement supplied pursuant to the 1992 Act permits the employer to refer an employee to a document, such as a collective agreement, as being the source of certain terms of the contract of employment.

A collective agreement may also expressly become part of a contract of employment by virtue of statutory provisions. There are a number of situations where this is possible:

a) under the 1992 Act. Provision is made for application to be made to the Secretary of State for the approval of dismissals procedures agreements. Such agreements, which replace the right to claim unfair dismissal for those employees covered, form part of the terms of employment of those employees within their ambit;

b) under the 1992 Act, a collective agreement may be made which substitutes for the right to claim a redundancy payment under the provisions of the 1996 Act, a right to claim under the collective agreement If such an agreement is approved by the Secretary of State, it forms part of the terms of employment of those employees to whom it applies;

c) under of the 1992 Act a collective agreement may be made which substitutes for the right to a guarantee payment under the provisions of the 1996 Act, a right to claim under the collective agreement. It should be noted that where the terms of a collective agreement are expressly incorporated and varied by consent between the unions and employers the new terms become incorporated into the individual contracts of employment; however, unilateral variation or abrogation of the agreement by one party does not have a corresponding effect on individual employment contracts;(Robertson and Jackson v British Gas (1983).

Works rule-books

A works rulebook can take a number of forms in so far as it may consist of an actual book given to each employee when he enters employment or at some subsequent date. These rules relate to disciplinary action, suspension, dismissal for conduct etc. Safety procedures are normally incorporated. S3 of the Employment Rights Act 1996 states that an employer must give details of disciplinary and grievance procedures to an employee when taking up employment.

As far as the effect on contract goes, if the employer gives the employee the rulebook, or expressly refers to it before a contract is signed then it is considered to be part of the contract. In Petrie v Macfisheries (1940) a notice was posted on the wall of the work place stating the circumstances in which sick pay would be paid. The plaintiff claimed that it was not part of his contract. The defendant's case was upheld as the rule concerning sick pay was deemed to be incorporated into his contract as a result of his continued working at the place.

Not all works rules will be part of the contract, particularly where there are numerous rules contained in the relevant documentation, some for example may be out of date and inappropriate. This is well illustrated by the decision in Secretary of State for Employment v ASLEF (1972) a case concerning the rule book of British Rail, where Lord Denning said ' Each man signs a form saying that he will abide by the rules but these rules are in no way terms of the contract of employment. They are only instructions to a man as to how to do his work'.

Custom

Custom plays a significant part in employment law. It seems that there are four different categories of custom, which may form part of a contract of employment.

a) Custom of a particular place of work.

b) Custom of an industry or trade.

c) Custom of a specific geographical locality.

d) Customary conduct of the parties to the contract of employment.

a) See Marshall v English Electric !1945)

b) See Sagar v Ridehalgh (1931) and Davson v France (1959)

c) Sagar v Ridehalgh

d) Mears v Safecar Security (1982)

Implied duties of the employee

Into every contract of employment are implied a number of obligations in so far as these are not inconsistent with the express terms of the individual contract of employment. These duties are based on principles developed by the courts in the decided cases.

Implied duties may be classified as follows:

a) to be willing and ready to work;

b) to use reasonable care and skill;

c) to obey lawful orders;

d) to take care of the employers property;

e) to act in good faith.

To be ready and willing to work

The fundamental duty owed to an employer by an employee is to be turn up to work and to work at the direction of the employer in return for wages. Two interesting cases have arisen in relation to this. Miles v Wakefield Metropolitan District Council (1987). M was a superintendent registrar of Births deaths and marriages, working 37 hours per week, three of which were on Saturday morning. As part of industrial action, M refused to carry out marriages on Saturday mornings, although he was willing to do his other work. Wages were deducted, M sued for lost wages and the employer won, with the House of Lords saying that where an employee refuses to perform the full range of duties and had been told that he would not be paid if he did not, then the employers were entitled to withhold the whole of his remuneration, (3Hrs) although he attended for work and carried out a substantial part of his duties.

To use reasonable care and skill

This has two aspects:

a) The duty not to be unduly negligent.

b) The duty to be reasonably competent.

If an employee is negligent during the course of his work, he may be regarded as being in breach of contract. In Lister v Romford Ice and Cold Storage Ltd (1957) a lorry driver, employed by the company, carelessly reversed his lorry and injured a fellow employee, who was his father. The employers paid damages to the father but claimed indemnity from the son, because of negligence. This was held to be the case.

Duty to be reasonably competent

If an employee is incompetent this may be a breach of contract. In Hamer v Cornelius (1858) this was held to be the case.

To obey lawful orders

An employee is under a duty to obey all the lawful orders of his employer, i.e. those which are within the scope of the contract. In Price v Mouat (1862) a lace salesman was ordered to card (pack) lace but he refused and was dismissed without notice. He claimed wrongful dismissal and this was held because the order was not one which was within the scope of his contract.

An employee, therefore, is not obliged to do any act which is deemed to fall outside the ambit of his individual contract of employment. The question of the introduction of new technology has caused problems here and must be linked to the scope of managerial prerogative in introducing new work techniques. In Cresswell v Board of Inland Revenue (1984) the Revenue wished to introduce a computer system to assist with the PAYE system. The majority of the work associated with the system had been done manually. Did the employers have the ability to change the nature of the working system. Did the employers have the ability to change the nature of the working system? Held: employees were expected to adopt the new methods and techniques in performing their contracts if the employer provided the necessary training in new skills.

To take care of employers property

An employer is under an obligation to take reasonable care of his employer's property. In Superflux v Plaisted (1958) the defendant had been in charge of a team of vacuum cleaner salesmen and had negligently allowed fourteen cleaners to be stolen from his van. Held: he was in breach of his contract of employment.

To act in good faith

This implied duty has several different aspects, which together form the basis of a relationship of trust. There is the duty not to make a secret profit, i.e. not to accept bribes. This principal was clear from the case of Reading v AG (1951) which concerned a member of the armed forces, in which Lord Normand said:

---though the relation of a member of his majesty's forces is not accurately described as that of a servant under a contract of service--he owes to the Crown a duty as full fiduciary as the duty of a servant to his master--and in consequence--all profits and advantages gained by the use of his military status are to be for the benefit of the Crown'.

Duty to disclose certain information.

There appears to be no general duty on an employee to inform his employer of his misconduct and deficiencies: Bell v Lever Brothers (1932). However, there is one important exception, namely where the employment of that particular person is made more hazardous by virtue of an undisclosed defect on part of the employee.

Covenants in restraint of trade

A covenant in restraint of trade is a clause in a contract, which purports to limit an employees rights to seek employment when and where he chooses upon leaving his employment. This is usually done as a protective measure by an employer when he might suffer as a result of disclosure of confidential information or for other such reasons.

There are difficulties however, in enforcing such covenants and the employer has to demonstrate that the covenant is justified. A court will look at such factors as time that the covenant runs, geographical area that it covers and public interest when considering the reasonableness of such covenants.

If a covenant is found to be unreasonable, the contract as a whole is not necessarily regarded as void, unless it is impossible to distinguish the covenant from the rest of the contract. If the covenant can be severed from the rest of the contract, without altering the nature of the agreement, the unreasonable clause may be struck out: see Commercial Plastics LTD v Vincent (1965).

If an employer breaks the contract of employment by wrongfully dismissing an employee, the employee may disregard any covenant in the contract which purports to limit his right to seek employment elsewhere: see General Billposting v Atkinson (1909).

Patents

At common law, unless the contract dealt with the matter, an employee would not normally be entitled to the benefit of any invention made by him if to allow him to do so would be a contravention of the implied duty of the employee to act in good faith. The Patents Act 1977, ss-39-47, gives ownership of an invention to the employee inventor unless the invention was made in the course of the duties for which he was employed. Any disputes are dealt with by the patents court.

Duties of the employer

By virtue of common law, and a number of statutory provisions, employers have a considerable number of obligations towards employees. The main examples are:

a) to pay contractually agreed remuneration

An employer is under no obligation to provide work as long as re-numeration is paid. This however, has been questioned in recent times, particularly in relation to skilled employees. Lord Denning said, in

48

Langston v AUEW (1973): 'in these days an employer, when employing a skilled man, is bound to provide him with work. By which I mean that the man should be given the opportunity of doing his work when it is available and when he is ready and willing to do it'. Therefore, a failure to provide work of a nature that the employee is used to could be regarded as constructive dismissal.

There are three exceptions to the rule, one is piecework, the second is where the nature of the employment is such that the actual performance of the work forms part of the consideration supplied by the employer, the employee may be entitled to compensation over and above the contractual wages. These situations are sometimes referred to as 'names in lights' clauses. the other exception is when an employee is taking part in limited industrial action.

National Minimum Wage

From April 1999 the amount of pay an employee is entitled to receive is governed by the National Minimum Wage Act (NMW) 1998. The Act by s.1 covers worker's which is wider than the traditional definition of employee in employment law. Essentially, the NMW will apply to a workers gross pay, which will include incentive payments. Certain other benefits will be excluded from the calculation, such as tips.

In March 2003, the Low Pay Commission stated that the main adult rate for workers aged 22 and over will be £4.20 per hour increasing to £4.50 per hour from October 2003. The rate for worker 18-22 is £3.60 per hour increasing to £3.80 per hour from October 2003. The development rate can also apply to workers aged 22 or over during their first six months in a new job with a new employer and who are receiving accredited training.

The above figures are correct at the time of writing. For up to date figures and other information concerning the NMW contact ACAS or the DTI. through their website.

Provisions relating to sick pay

An employer may have an obligation by virtue of a term in the contract of employment to pay sick pay to employees. Such an obligation may arise as a result of an express term or an obligation may arise under an implied term. The principles governing the implication of terms relating to sick pay were discussed by the court of appeal in Mears v Safecar Security Ltd (1982) where it was held that there is no general presumption of an implied right to sick pay.

Since April 1983 all employers have had a statutory obligation under the Social Security and Housing Benefits Act 1982 to pay Statutory Sick Pay to their employees. The employer pays the employee his statutory sick pay and, until recently then recouped those payments through his National Insurance Contributions.

By the Statutory Sick Pay Act 1994 only those employers who pay less than £2000 in National Insurance contributions can now recoup such payments.

In outline the scheme provides that a qualifying employee is entitled to SSP for the first 28 weeks of sickness and after that period he will receive state sickness benefit. Certain employees are excluded from the scheme, including pensioners, persons employed for less than three months, persons who do not pay NI contributions and persons who are not employed due to a trade union dispute at their workplace.

b) to treat employees with trust and confidence

In Courtaulds Northern Textiles Ltd v Andrew (1978) the EAT held'--- there is an implied term in a contract of employment that employers will not, without reasonable and proper cause, conduct themselves in a manner calculated or likely to destroy or seriously damage the relationship of trust or confidence between the parties' A series of cases have firmly established this principle.

c) to observe provisions relating to holidays

The written statement provided to employees under the 1996 Act ought to state the holidays to which the employee is entitled and whether the employee is entitled to holiday pay and if so how much. There are relatively few statutory provisions. Section 94 of the Factories Act 1961 provides that women and young persons who work in factories must have a holiday on bank holidays and the Wages Councils and Agricultural Wages Board have the power to fix holiday pay for workers in the industries over which they have jurisdiction.

d) to observe provisions relating to hours of work

The hours which an employee is required to work, are determined by reference to his individual contract of employment and the written statement supplied to the employee ought to state these. There are certain statutory provisions, section 7 of the Sex Discrimination Act 1986 removes the majority of limitations imposed concerning the hours to be worked by women. Part V1 of the Factories Act 1961 limits the working day to no more than nine hours for young people.

In addition, see below, the Working Time Regulations 1998. These have introduced specific regulations controlling the working week and covers a broad variety of workers not only employees.

e) to permit employees time off work for public duties

The 1996 Act provides that an employer must permit an employee to have time off work for the purpose of carrying out work as:

a) Justice of the peace (work relating to this)

b) a member of a local authority

c) a member of a statutory tribunal

d) a member of a regional health authority or an Area or District educational establishment.

e) a member of a governing body of a local authority maintained educational establishment.

A number of categories of employees are excluded from this right, under the 1996 Act.

Under the 1996 Act a pregnant employee has the right not to be unreasonably refused time off work with pay in order that she may keep appointments for receiving anti-natal care. Evidence of pregnancy and appointment must be produced if requested by employer.

f) to indemnify employees

An employer is under an obligation to indemnify his employees in respect of any expenses incurred in performing their duties under the contract of employment, for example travelling expenses.

In certain circumstances however, the employee may be under an obligation to indemnify the employer for any loss sustained: see Lister v Romford Ice and Cold Storage LTD (1957)

h) to provide references

There is no obligation on an employer to supply character references for employees although, in practice, employers normally supply them since failure to provide one speaks for itself. The legal effect of references means that if an employer does provide one, it ought to be correct for several reasons:

a) defamation. If a reference is defamatory, the defamed employee may bring an action against the employer, although the defence of qualified privilege is available to the employer, i.e. the employer may show that the statements were made without malice.

b) negligent misstatement. A person who acts in reliance on a reference, which has been issued negligently, may apparently bring an action to recover any loss sustained as a consequence.

i) to insure employees and other duties.

The Working Time Regulations 1998

The Working Time Regulations have been brought in to implement the EU Working Time Directive (No 93/104/EC) and the Young Workers Directive (No 94/33/EC). The Regulations came into force on the 1st October 1998. The regulations cover workers as a wider group rather than employees. The limit imposed on the working week is 48hrs. This, however, is a limit on average working time, the average being calculated over a reference period of 17 weeks. An individual may opt out of the 48 hour week, by agreement. The Regulations also cover rest breaks and periods, night work and annual leave. By Regulation 10, adult workers are entitled to at least 11 consecutive hours rest in each 24 hour period. (12 hours for workers under 18). Shift workers are exempt when they change shift or the shift involves periods of work split up over the day provided they are given equivalent periods of rest. Workers are also entitled to an uninterrupted weekly rest period of no fewer than 24 hours (48 hours if under 18) in each seven day period averaged over 14 days and are entitled to rest breaks during the day where the working time is more than six hours. The break should be negotiated by collective or workforce agreement, but if none is in force, should be for an uninterrupted period of not less than 20 minutes.

In respect of night workers (workers working between 11pm and 6am) Regulation 6 specifies that the normal working hours should not exceed an average of eight in any 24hr period. The 17-week reference period is used to calculate the average. If the work involves special hazards or heavy strain, working hours must not exceed eight in any 24 hour period. In addition, the employer must give the worker the opportunity of a free health assessment before starting night work and regular assessments thereafter. If a night worker is suffering from health problems which are connected with night work, he or she is entitled to be transferred whenever possible to day work.

All workers, after a 13-week qualifying period, are be entitled to three weeks holiday, paid, each year, rising to four weeks from November 1999. This is subject to the employee giving the employer twice as much notice as the leave they want to take.

Regulation 18 excludes certain workers from the general provisions, doctors in training, police and armed forces and certain sector activities such as air, rail, road and sea. Regulation 21 also excludes certain kinds of workers, such as service workers, gas and electricity, water and others.

3

REMUNERATION

Remuneration

A number of legislative provisions exist affecting remuneration to employees and the way it is paid, the 1970 Equal Pay Act, The Wages Act 1986, consolidated by the 1996 Employment Rights Act and the National Minimum Wage Act 1998. (See previous chapter for a more detailed discussion of the NMW Act). In addition, the 2002 Employment Act has introduced changes to rights of parents and their remuneration. See below.

The scope of the Acts is wide. By S8 of the 1996 Act every employee who works eight hours or more a week has the right to an itemised pay statement. It must state the gross and net amount of pay and the amounts deducted and the purpose of the deduction.

The 1970 Equal pay Act provides that all employees doing the same job be paid equal wages or salary. However, surprisingly, the Act does not include a right for an applicant to serve a questionnaire upon its employer in order to elicit information as to whether or not they are receiving equal pay.

S.42 of the EA 2002 will insert a provision into the Equal pay Act 1970 which will allow applicants to issue questionnaires in the same way as they can in race or sex discrimination cases. Whilst employers will not be obliged to answer the questionnaire, a Tribunal hearing the case is entitled to draw adverse inferences from a failure to answer where answers are evasive or equivocal.

The 1986 Wages Act, now consolidated by the 1996 Act defined wages in very broad terms. Wages means 'any sum payable to a worker by his employer in connection with his employment and includes any fee, bonus commission, holiday pay or other emolument referable to his employment, whether payable under his contract or otherwise...' However, a number of payments are specifically excluded and these include expenses and redundancy payments.

One of the effects of the 1986 Wages Act was to abolish the requirement that workers be paid in 'coin of the realm'. We now have the concept of cash-less pay. The 1996 Act only allows deductions from wages if it is made by virtue of a statutory provision or by a provision of the workers contract, or if the work has previously indicated his agreement in writing to it. There are much stricter controls on retail workers who are defined as being workers who carry out retail transactions directly with members of the public or with fellow workers. Under the Act any deductions in respect of cash shortages or stock deficiencies must not exceed one tenth of the gross amount of wages payable on that day. Also, any sum demanded of such a worker in respect of these losses shall not exceed the 10% figure.

Guarantee payments

Unless a contract of employment expressly or implicitly allows for it, an employee who is laid off is entitled to be paid during the period of such lay off. To be eligible to receive such a payment, an employee must:

a) have been continuously employed for at least one month when the lay off occurs;
b) have been laid off for the whole of his working hours on a day he is normally required to work;
c) not have unreasonably refused an offer of alternative employment, which was suitable in all the circumstances;
d) have complied with any reasonable requirements imposed by the employer with a view to ensuring that his services are available;
e) not have been laid off because of a strike, lock out or other industrial action involving any employee of the employer or of any associated employer; and
f) have been available for employment on that day.

An employee who is entitled to a guarantee payment is entitled to be paid at the guaranteed hourly rate, subject to a maximum limit for one day. There is a maximum entitlement of five guarantee payments in any period of three months.

Suspension from work on medical grounds

For the legislation governing suspension from work on medical grounds, ss 19-22 of the 1978 Act as amended by the Employment Act 1982 and see also Protection (medical suspension) Order 1985 (these were consolidated by the Employment Rights Act 1996 and s 64 now deals).

The above Act provides that an employee who is suspended from work is entitled to be paid by his employer if that suspension is in consequence of a requirement imposed under certain statutory provisions or a recommendation made in a Code of Practice issued or approved under s 16 of the Health and safety at Work Act 1974. There are certain eligibility criteria concerning length of employment etc. An employee is entitled to be paid for up to twenty-six weeks of such suspension.

Maternity and Parental pay and leave

Apart from important protection from unfair dismissal because of pregnancy, the Employment Rights Act 1996 provided four further protections in relation to pregnancy - the right to maternity leave, the right to return to work after maternity leave, the right to time off for ante-natal care and the right to maternity pay. The section of the above Act dealing with maternity leave was replaced in its entirety by the Employment Relations Act 1999 Part 1, Schedule 4 which in turn has been amended by the 2002 Employment Act, the provisions of which came into force on April 6th 2003.

Right to maternity leave

The EC Pregnancy Directive (Council Directive 92/85/EEC) regulates maternity leave and is implemented by the 1996 Employment Rights Act and the 1999 Employment Relations Act as amended by the 2002 Employment Act. The Directive gives all pregnant employees a general right to maternity leave.

Under the 1999 Employment Rights Act, which came into force on the 15th December 1999, the periods of leave were renamed. Maternity leave became ordinary maternity leave (OML) and additional absence became additional maternity leave (AML).

The regulations now clarify that the term remuneration is now limited to 'sums payable by way of wages or salary'. This means, for example, that women will automatically be entitled to retain a company car and a mobile phone and to receive a performance bonus which is not salary.

The period of the paid leave (OML) is now 26 weeks under the Employment Act 2002. This is available to all employees from the first day of employment. The employer must be informed at least 21 days before leave commences that she intends to exercise her rights, and of the date her absence will commence and must be either in writing or oral if the employer requires. The employer can request a certificate of proof of pregnancy and expected date of birth.

Additional Maternity Leave is available for a further 26 weeks after the expiry of the initial 26 weeks OML. The qualifying period for this new Additional maternity leave is the same as Statutory Maternity pay, i.e. the employee must have 26 weeks service with their employer by the time they have reached 15 weeks before the EWC (expected week of childbirth).

If the employee has already a contractual right to maternity pay/leave, she may exercise her right to the more favourable. If there is a redundancy situation during the leave period and it is not practicable because of the redundancy for the employer to continue to employ her under her existing contract, she is entitled to be offered a suitable vacancy before her employment ends.

If a woman intends to return to work before the end of maternity leave, 21 days notice must be given.

Since women who qualify now have the right to take Additional Maternity Leave, and there is no obligation to notify the employer during the initial notification, then until notification of a return to work is given, the women will retain the right to return but not pay.

Time off for ante-natal care

To qualify for this right the employee must have made an appointment for ante-natal care on the advice of a doctor, midwife or health visitor. The employer may not refuse time off for the first visit, but for further appointments, the employer may ask for a certificate or appointment card or other evidence.

Statutory maternity pay

The Social Security Act of 1996 and the Statutory Maternity Pay regulations of the same year entitle certain employees to statutory maternity pay. This has been amended by the 2002 Employment Act in that there has been an increase in the standard rate of Statutory Maternity pay (SMP) to £100 per week or to 90% of wages if this is lower. (Check current amounts as these are the amounts applicable 2003/2004.. If the employee has been working for the employer for 26 weeks by the 15th week before the expected week of confinement, she is entitled to SMP for 18 weeks. She is entitled to nine tenths of her pay for the first six weeks of the 18 and the higher rate of Statutory Sick Pay for the further 18.

Insolvency of employer

For the legislation governing the insolvency of an employer, the Employment Rights Act 1996 applies. See also s 175 and schedule 6 of the Insolvency Act 1986. If an employer becomes insolvent an employee acquires certain rights. He becomes a preferential creditor in respect of up to four months-unpaid wages or a maximum set by the Secretary of State. Certain other payments are also deemed to be preferential debts including guarantee payments, payment for time off for trade union activities and payment for ante -natal care. The employee is entitled to claim payments of certain amounts due to him from his employer from the Secretary of State who will pay them out of the redundancy fund. The classes of debt for which payment may be made include arrears of wages (up to a maximum of 8 weeks) holiday pay (6 weeks) and wages during the statutory minimum notice period.

Parental leave

The Maternity and Parental Leave Regulations 1999 provide that every person who cares for a young child, or has recently adopted a child, can take time off from work at his or her own convenience to care for that child. Minimum provisions are set for leave, preconditions are set for leave and the notice that an employee has to give an employer before leave can be taken is set out. Employers and employees can agree to vary these provisions by using a workforce agreement as long as it is equal to or more favourable than the statutory provisions.

Any employee who has one years continuous employment at the date the leave is due to start, and who has, or expects to have, responsibility for a child at that time can apply to take parental leave. A person will have responsibility for a child under the regulations if he/she has parental responsibility under the Children Act 1989 or is registered as the father under the provision of the Births and Deaths Register Act. Each employee is entitled to take up to 13 weeks of unpaid parental leave in respect of each child born after, or placed for adoption after, 15th December 1999. In addition, the 2002 Employment Act has widened the scope and range of paternity leave, The Act has introduced the right to two weeks paid leave in addition to the 13 weeks unpaid leave. This became effective from April 2003. Leave must be taken within 8 weeks of the birth of the child or placement of the child through adoption. Statutory Paternity Pay (SPP) will be paid at the rate of either £100 per week or 90% of earnings whichever is lower.

Employees will only be entitled to claim paternity leave if they have been with their employer for 26 weeks

- by the 15th week before the Expected Week of Childbirth (EWC) (in the case of birth) or,
- by the 26th week before the date of the placement for adoption

Structure of paternity leave

Paternity leave can be taken as a single block of either one or two weeks. The definition of who qualifies for paternity leave is wide ranging and covers:
- the biological father
- someone who is married to the mother or to the 'adoptor' or
- someone who is the partner of the mother (or the adoptor) in an enduring relationship

This is much wider than was originally anticipated and could cover homosexual couples. All terms and conditions of employment remain intact during the period of paternity leave except the right to remuneration. Employees are entitled to return to the jobs they had before they took paternity leave.

Adoption leave and pay

The 2002 Employment Act creates a right for parents to take adoption leave when permanently adopting a child. An adoptive parent will be entitled to take 26 weeks paid adoption leave (known as 'ordinary adoption leave') and up to 26 weeks unpaid adoption leave (this will be know as 'additional adoption leave') During ordinary adoption leave, employees will be entitled to receive Statutory Adoption pay (SAP) of £100 per week or 90% of earnings, whichever is the lower.

Qualifying requirements

To be entitled to take adoption leave, employees must have attained 26 weeks service with their employer at the date the adoption takes place. Leave can be taken at any time after the adoption placement begins. Employees will be required to provide evidence of the adoption to the employer. Only one partner in a couple will be able to take adoption leave. The other partner, male or female, will be able to take paternity leave for 2 weeks and receive SPP. There are statutory notice provisions covering how and when employees must inform employers that they wish to take adoption leave. These are flexible and can be verified with the employer. During the period of ordinary adoption leave the employee is entitled to all their terms and conditions, except the right to remuneration. During the period of additional adoption leave, the employee is in the same position as someone on additional maternity leave – namely that whilst most of the terms and conditions of employment will be suspended, those relating to notice, confidentiality, implied terms of mutual trust and confidence, redundancy terms and disciplinary and grievance procedures will remain in place.

The right to return after either ordinary or additional adoption leave mirror's the provisions for ordinary and additional maternity leave respectively.

New statutory right to request a contractual variation

The 2002 Employment Act introduces a right to request a contractual variation, where the reason for the request relates to a young child. Applications can only be made by parents whose children are under 6 at the time of the application or by parents of disabled children under the age of 18. An employee can request changes to his or her terms and conditions and, in particular, the following:

- Hours of work
- The times when the employee is required to work.
- Where the employee is required to work
- Such other aspect of his or her terms and conditions of employment as the Secretary of State may specify

Procedure for flexible working request

A request for flexible working must:

- State that it is a request for flexible working'
- Specify the changes applied for and the date on which they are to become effective and:
- Explain what effect the changes have on the workplace and how they can propose they can be dealt with

Only one request can be made per year.

Employer's response

The employer must consider the application and can only refuse the application on certain given grounds. These are as follows:

- The burden of additional costs
- The detrimental effect on ability to meet customer demand
- The inability to reorganize work amongst existing staff
- The detrimental impact on quality
- The detrimental impact on performance
- The insufficiency of work during the period the employee proposes to work: and
- Any planned structural changes

Regulations will provide a timetable detailing how the employer must respond to a request for flexible working. It is likely that an employer will be required to arrange a meeting to consider the request within 28 days of receipt. The employer must give a decision within 14 days of the meeting. If the employee's request is refused, the employer must give grounds for the decision. An employee will be entitled to appeal but must set out their grounds for appeal. The employer must hear the appeal within 14 days and a decision must be given to the employee within 14 days of the appeal hearing.

Remedies

Where a request has been refused an employee can bring a claim at the Employment Tribunal but only where the employer:

- Has failed to comply with the statutory procedure in considering the application.
- Has refused the request on a ground that is different to the specified grounds above: or
- Has made the decision based on incorrect facts
- Therefore, there is no jurisdiction for the Employment Tribunal to hear a claim if the employee is merely unhappy about the decision.

If the Tribunal finds against the employer it can:

- Order reconsideration of the issue and/or
- Make an award for compensation

In addition, there will also be the right for employees not to be subjected to a detriment, including dismissal by the employer if they have made an application for flexible working, they have appealed against a refusal to allow flexible working, they have brought proceedings in the Employment Tribunal in respect of a refusal to allow flexible working, or the employee has alleged circumstances which could constitute a ground for bringing such proceedings.

Part Time Workers

There have been significant advances relating to the position of part time workers in relation to remuneration and terms and conditions of employment. The Part-Time Workers (Prevention of Less Favourable Treatment) Regulations 2000 introduced new rights for part-time workers. The Part-Time Workers Regulations ensure that Britain's part timers are not treated less favourably than comparable full-timers in their terms and conditions, unless it is objectively justified. This means part-timers are entitled to a range of benefits, including:

- The same hourly rates of pay
- The same access to company pension schemes
- The same entitlements to annual leave and maternity/parental leave on a pro-rata basis
- The same entitlement to contractual sick pay
- No less favourable treatment in access to training

Two recent amendments in 2002 have introduced Comparators and occupational pension schemes (regulation 2).

Under the original regulations, part-timers had to compare themselves to full-timers employed under the same type of contract. This meant that, for example a part-timer on a fixed-term contract should compare themselves to a full-timer on a fixed-term contract. This is no longer the case

The other amendment is that of access to occupational pension schemes. Under Regulation 8 (8) of the Part Time Workers Regulations, where an employment Tribunal has upheld a complaint from a part timer for equal access to an occupational pension scheme, the remedies which the tribunal orders may go back no further than two years. In 2001, the House of Lords held that this was unlawful in that it contravened European law on the equal treatment of men and women, and could no longer be maintained. As a consequence the law has now been amended to remove the two-year time limit.

4

Trade Unions

The statutory definition of a trade union is now found in s1 (a) of the Trade Union and Labour relations (Consolidation) Act 1992 that provides that a trade union means:

"an organisation (whether temporary or permanent) which consists wholly or mainly of workers of one or more descriptions and whose principle purposes includes the regulations of relations between workers of that description or those descriptions and employers or employers associations."

The definition is wide and concentrates on the purpose of that body. Thus a body which had a subsidiary purpose of regulating relations between workers and employers would not be a trade union. In Midland Cold Storage v Turner, 1972, a shop stewards committee drawn from various trade unions was not a trade union within the definition since its purpose was to discuss whether industrial action should be taken and it did not engage in negotiation with employers.

Listing

The concept of maintaining some kind of voluntary listing of trade unions was introduced by the Trade Union Act 1871. Such a list continued with the compliance of the unions until the Industrial Relations Act 1971 that introduced a very different system of registration. Under that Act, only unions who registered were entitled to statutory immunity against certain industrial action. In addition, any unions who registered under the 1971 Act had to 'pay' for their immunity by subjecting their constitution, rules and accounts to outside scrutiny.

Union opposition to the Act demonstrated itself by a policy of non-compliance and very few unions registered. Those that did were expelled from the TUC. The Trade Unions and Labour Relations Act 1974, which repealed the 1971 Act reintroduced the concept of voluntary listing similar to that under the 1871 Act. The provisions are now in s 2 and 123 of the Trade Union and Labour Relations (Consolidation) Act 1992. These provide that the Certification Officer shall maintain a voluntary list of trade unions and employers associations.

Whilst there are few advantages to being listed, it is the first requisite to obtaining a certificate of independence. This certificate brings considerable advantages.

Independent Trade Unions

The Certification Officer can issue any union on the list with a certificate of independence. Such a certificate is conclusive evidence that a union is independent. An independent union is one which is not under the control of an employer or liable to interference from an employer arising out of financial, material or other support. This definition was elaborated in the Court of Appeal and Squib UK Staff Association v Certification officer (1979).

Recognition of Trade Unions

The major purpose of any union is to protect and promote its members interests and the way it will do this is by collective bargaining. Recognised Trade Unions have certain rights. Recognised Trade Unions are entitled to information for collective bargaining purposes. Although there is now no formal way that a union can demand recognition from an employer, recognition procedures having been abolished by the Employment Act 1980, and the 1999 Employment Rights Act has introduced a new right where, if a majority of staff are in favour of joining a union, then an employer must recognize that union in the workplace

The above discussion raises the question of when is a union recognised?. The starting point is the statutory definition in s 178 (3) of the 1992 Act which defines recognition as 'recognition of the union by the employer....to any extent, for the purposes of collective bargaining.. However, this is vague and unhelpful and does not constitute formal recognition. Despite Article 15 of the European Social Charter which takes the position that collective bargaining should be promoted, it seems a long way off. The present Trade Union Reform and Employment Rights Act 1993 removes the statutory duty of ACAS to encourage the extension, development and reform of collective bargaining.

The Political Fund

The labour movement in the early years was reliant on a sympathetic Liberal Government to give it legal protection. While this partnership worked well, it soon became apparent that the movement required working class MPs who would fully understand the problems and provide true representation in Parliament. As such the movement decided to fund such MPs through union funds. This subsidy was declared illegal by the House of Lords and again a sympathetic liberal government came to the unions rescue with the passage of the Trade Unions Act 1913. Substantial amendments were made to the Act by the Trade Union Act 1984, although at the time the government renounced its intention of reintroducing the contracting-in system but insisted that unions ballot their members every ten years to see if the members wished the political fund to be maintained.

The Trade Union Reform and Employment Rights Act 1993, however, introduced the contracting-in system. Section 68 of the 1992 Act now provides that an employer shall not deduct union subscriptions from a workers wages unless the worker has authorised the deduction in writing within the past three years, the employer has notified the worker of any increases at least one month before the deduction is made and the employer has notified the employee of his right to withdraw his authorization at any time.

The 1993 Act also introduced stringent balloting procedures in relation to the maintenance of a political fund, requiring such ballots to be conducted in the same way as the ballot for the election of trade union officials.

The present law is contained in the 1992 Trade Union and Labour Relations (Consolidation) Act 1992. Section 71(1) lays down that payment for political purposes whether made directly or indirectly can be made only from a separate political fund.

Political Purposes are then defined in Section 72(1) as the expenditure of money:

a) on any contribution to the funds of, or on the payment of expenses incurred directly or indirectly, by a political party;

b) on the provisions of any service or property for use by or on behalf of any political party;

c) in connection with the registration of electors, the candidature of any person, the selection of any candidate or the holding of any ballot by the union in connection with any election to a political office;

d) on the maintenance of any holder of a political office;

e) on the holding of any conference by or on behalf of a political party or of any other meeting the purpose of which is the transaction of business in connection with a political party;

f) on the production, publication or distribution of any literature, document, film, sound recording or advertisement the main purpose of which is to persuade people to vote for a political party or candidate or persuade them not to vote for a political party or candidate.

The 1992 Act lays down conditions for the establishment and maintenance of a political fund. A political resolution must be passed by a majority of members voting on a ballot conducted according to the provisions of the act, that is, it must comply with the political ballot rules as approved by the certification officer. The Certification Officer cannot approve such rules unless they include the appointment of an independent scrutineer, entitlement of all the members to vote and the rules provide for a scrutineers report.

The Rule Book

The rules of a trade union form the terms of a contract between it and its members. They become part of a contract in the same way that collective agreements become part of the individuals employment contract between the employer and the employee. Apart from contract, other areas of law impact on the union rulebook. Statute has now impacted in a variety of ways. By s69 of the Trade Union and Labour Relations (Consolidation) Act 1992, for example, there is a rule in all union rule books allowing a member to terminate his membership on the giving of reasonable notice.

In addition, both the Sex Discrimination Act 1975 and the Race Relations Act 1976 render it unlawful to discriminate on the grounds of race or sex, in relation to membership.

The Right to Information

The Employment Protection Act 1975 recognised that to be able to collectively bargain effectively, unions needed certain information from the employer and as such the Act introduced a right to receive certain information. This right has been retained and the provisions are now ss 181-5 of the Trade union and Labour Relations (Consolidation) Act 1992. The employer only has to disclose information in relation to those matters for which the union is recognised for collective bargaining.

ACAS has produced a code of practice (ACAS Code of Practice 2: Disclosure of information to Trade Unions for Collective Bargaining Purposes) which in paragraph 11 lists the type of information it would be good industrial relations practice to disclose. This includes pay and benefits, conditions of service, manpower, performance and financial information. Section 182 of the Act provides restrictions on information that the employer does not have to disclose, such as information in the interests of national security. Section 183 provides a remedy for a trade union where the employer has failed to provide information. The remedy is complaint to the Central Arbitration Committee (CAC). Sections 184-185 further strengthen the complaints procedure.

The Closed Shop

There was no legal control over the closed shop until the Industrial Relations Act 1971. This Act introduced the concept of unfair dismissal. In 1988, the Employment Act 1988 rendered any dismissal for union or non-union membership unfair in any circumstances (now s 152 of the Trade Union and Labour Relations (consolidation) Act 1992.

As such, while post-entry closed shops can still exist, no one can be legally compelled to join a union.

The legislation of 1988 however, did nothing to prevent pre-entry closed shops operating, pre-entry meaning insistence on membership of a union before being offered employment. The Employment Act 1990 finally destroyed any protection which existed for the pre entry closed shop by rendering it illegal to discriminate on the grounds of membership of a union prior to employment. This is now Ss 137-1243 of the Trade Union and Labour Relations (Consolidation) Act 1992.

THE RIGHTS OF TRADE UNION MEMBERS

Enforcement of the Rule Book

While there is a special statutory protection for union members in relation to rules relating to discipline and exclusion and expulsion a member must rely on the common law to enforce any other rule in the rulebook. Although the rulebook forms the contract of membership between the individual member and union, this will not always provide him with a remedy. Rather, the trade union member is treated in a similar way to a shareholder in a company and as such his remedies against the union are similar to those imposed against incorporated associations.

The simple proposition is that, as a union as an entity only exists as a creation of statute, its legal capacity to act comes from its rules and to some extent from statute. As such, if the rules or statute lay down when a union can act then should the union act without fulfilling the requirements it has no capacity to do so and as such its actions are ultra vires.

Exclusion and Expulsion

We have already seen that essentially a trade union cannot legally enforce a closed shop and therefore it may appear that any discussion on exclusion and expulsion may be redundant.

Closed shops still exist, however, in certain industries and whereas the employee may have a remedy against the employer for refusing to employ him because he is not a trade union member, that will not help him if the reason he is not such a member is that the union do not want him or have expelled him.

Discipline of union members

Although expulsion from the union may be imposed as a disciplinary sanction, it is not the only form of sanction imposed by a union on its members. The courts insist however, that the union must comply with the natural rules of justice when exercising sanctions against a member. These are:

1. *Notice.* A person must be given adequate notice of the charge against him and the potential penalty so that he has an opportunity to answer it. In Annamunthodo v Oilfield Workers Union (1961) the plaintiff knew that he was being charged with making allegations against the union presidents and knew he could be fined. He did not know that such

conduct was treated as prejudicial to the union and that he could be expelled. It was held that his subsequent expulsion was void.

2. *Opportunity to put his case.* A person must be given the opportunity to put his side of the case and answer any charges against him.

3. *Unbiased hearing.* The hearing should be unbiased.

4. *Representation.* The rules do not specifically state that a person should be allowed legal representation and it appears from Enderby Town Football Club v Football Association (1971) that such representation can be specifically excluded by the rules as long as some kind of representative is allowed.

Commissioner for the Rights of Trade Union Members

The above office was created by the Employment Act 1988 and the provisions are now in the 1992 Act. The Commissioner may give assistance to individuals in the following Matters:

a) failure to hold a ballot before industrial action;

b) failure to permit members to inspect union accounts;

c) unlawful application of union property by trustees;

d) failure to maintain a register of members;

e) failure to comply with balloting provisions in relation to the political fund;

f) failure to bring or continue proceedings to recover property used to unlawfully indemnify an individual;

g) failure to comply with the balloting provisions in relation to the trade union elections;

h) application of union funds for unlawful political purposes;

i) alleged breaches of union rules in relation to appointment to any office, disciplinary proceedings, authorization or endorsement of industrial action, balloting, the application of the unions funds or property, the imposition or collection of levies for industrial action purposes and the constitution or proceedings of any committee, conference or body of the union.

Action Short of Dismissal

The law affords a certain amount of protection against an employer. The law protects an employee who is dismissed for trade union membership or non-membership or for taking part in trade union activities at the appropriate time. Protection against dismissal is complemented by protection against action short of dismissal for one of the above grounds and is now found in s146 of the Trade Union and Labour Relations (Consolidation) Act 1992. Should a tribunal find a complaint well founded it can make a declaration to that effect and award compensation to offset any loss caused by the action. In addition, either the complainant or the employer may join the union as a co-respondent if it was union pressure which induced the action and the tribunal can order that some or all of the compensation be paid by the union.

Refusal to grant a benefit on these grounds is action short of dismissal for the purposes of protection.

In NCB v Ridgeway (1987) it was held that refusal to giver a pay rise negotiated with the UDM to NUM Members was unlawful action short of dismissal. In other words it is sufficient if the employer discriminates against members of a particular union and it is not necessary to show discrimination against union members as a whole.

Industrial Action

The present law on industrial action has had a chequered history. For many years the law was, to a large extent, non-interventionist in this area. The main piece of legislation governing industrial action was the Trade Disputes Act 1906 which created the basic immunities.

Change came with the Conservative Government in the early 1970's. The Industrial Relations Act of 1971 introduced a system of registration for trade unions and attacked the closed shop. Since 1979, there have been a number of reforms, ten pieces of legislation in all.

Employment legislation overall is part of broader economic policy, that of the encouragement of market forces. Reduce the power of the unions and you remove the obstacles to competitiveness. Finally, the 1993 Labour Relations Act is the latest in a long line of legislation designed to weaken unions.

Industrial Action and the Contract of Employment

Virtually all forms of industrial action will constitute a breach of contract on the part of the employee. There are a number of forms, or types of industrial action.

Go Slow

A go-slow is a breach of an implied term to work at a reasonable pace in the absence of justifying circumstances.

Work to rule

The leading case of Secretary of State for Employment v Aslef (1972) decided that such an action could constitute a breach of contract, as the employees were following a rule book set out by the employer which did not constitute a contract.

Overtime ban

Whether this action constitutes a breach of contract depends on whether the overtime is compulsory or voluntary and involves looking at the terms of the contract itself.

Blacking

This may take a variety of forms. If a reasonable order is given by the employer however, and the employee refuses to undertake the work then this can be seen as breach of contract. Another form of blacking may constitute refusing to work with ones fellow employees. In Bowes and Partners v Press (1894) miners refused an order to go down in a cage with a non-unionist. It was held that their action was a breach of contract.

Strike without notice

A strike is a situation where an individual withdraws his labor and refuses to work. As such, he is in breach of contract by refusing to work.

Strike with notice

This area is complicated and a number of court cases have tried to determine whether a strike with notice is in fact breach of contract or resignation of the employee. One leading case is that of Miles v Wakefield Metropolitan District Council (1987) (House of Lords) where it was held that all industrial action is a repudiatory breach of contract since there is an intention to harm the employers business which goes fundamentally against the duty of loyalty and co-operation which the employee owes to the employer. If this view is correct and the intention behind the action is one of legality, it would suggest that any strike notice, whether of correct length or not is notice of a breach of contract and it will only be construed as notice to terminate if it is expressed to be so.

Trade Dispute

In terms of legal liabilities, it is of the utmost significance whether an act is done in contemplation or furtherance of a trade dispute' since the statutory immunities discussed below only apply in certain circumstances. If an act falls outside of a trade dispute, the immunities cease to operate and the full rigour of the law applies.

A trade dispute is defined as '... a dispute between workers and their employer which relates wholly or mainly to one or more of the following, that is to say:

a) terms and conditions of employment, or the physical condition in which any workers are required to work;

b) engagement or non engagement or termination or suspension or the duties of employment, of one or more workers;

c) allocation of work or the duties of employment as between workers or groups of workers;

d) matters of discipline

e) the membership or non membership of a trade union on the part of a worker;

f) facilities for officials of a trade union and

g) machinery for negotiation or consultation and other procedures, relating to any of the foregoing matters, including the recognition by employers or employers associations of the right of a trade union to represent workers in any such negotiations or consultation or in the carrying out of such procedures'.

The above definition was introduced in 1982 and the present definition is narrower in two broad respects:

a) it extends only to disputes between workers and their employers. It does not embrace disputes between workers and workers.

b) the dispute must relate wholly or mainly to one of the matters mentioned in the 1993 Act.

Industrial action and the economic torts

Inducement of a breach of contract

Since the passage of the Employment Act 1982, trade unions are no longer immune from suit in tort. If a person induces a party to break that contract, the injured party may sue the inducer in tort for inducement of a breach of contract. However, in order to be liable, the defendant must have induced an unlawful act. If the unlawful act is a breach of contract, the contract must exist and be valid in law at the time of inducement. (Long v Smithson) 1918.Knowledge and intention are also necessary requisites for an unlawful act.

Further, the concept of inducement is important here. The word inducement implies pressure being put on an unwilling party, but what amount of inducement does the law require? The key fact seems to be the intention of the person communicating, or the speaker and if that person intends that the contract be broken then there is an inducement even if the speaker is merely communicating a set of facts to the recipient of the information.

Intimidation

The basis of this tort is the use of unlawful threats to induce a party to commit a lawful act, which causes injury, classically, threatening industrial action which causes the employer to lawfully terminate an employees contract. The requirements of the tort are unlawful threats, intention to harm, causation and loss to the plaintiff.

Conspiracy

This tort consists of two forms, the first simple conspiracy to injure and the second to use unlawful means. The existence of a simple conspiracy was recognised in Mogul Steamship v Mcgregor and Co (1892) when the House of Lords stated that the tort had three elements: a combination of at least two persons; intentionally causing loss; and the predominant purpose is not to further a legitimate interest. In addition, there must be an agreement to injure, not just a co-incidental action. This is different to criminal conspiracy where the intention to cause loss forms the basis of the offence even if no loss occurs.

Interference with a trade or business by unlawful means

This tort was declared to exist by the Court of Appeal in Hadmor Productions Limited v Hamilton (1981). In Hadmor it was alleged that ACCT officials threatened to persuade their members to refuse to transmit television programmes produced by Hadmor. Thames Television had acquired a licence to transmit the programmes but was under no contractual obligation to do so. Therefore, Hadmor had no contract to breach in this case. It was held, however, that a tort existed. Although the essence of a tort is unlawful means an intention to harm a plaintiff can also be a tort.

Economic duress

All industrial action is intended to put pressure on the employer. In contact law, economic pressure can amount to duress and, if proved, the contract can be avoided and any money paid under it recovered. Normally this argument is not used against unions as they have no contract with the employer. However, in Universe Tankships of Monrovia v International Transport Workers Federation (1983) such a contract did exist. The Federation, as part of its campaign against flags of convenience, insisted that employers pay a sum into the union's welfare fund as the price for lifting the blacking of a ship. As soon as the blacking was lifted the employers sought to recover the money they had paid, arguing the payment had been made under duress and therefore was avoidable. The House of Lords said that if the action had been protected by the immunities, that is, if it was in contemplation or furtherance of a trade dispute, the employer could not circumvent the protection by bringing an action for duress. However, since payment into a welfare fund is not a recognised trade dispute, there was no such protection and the employer's action succeeded.

Statutory Immunities

It can be seen from the above that unions can commit a great number of economic torts when they take industrial action, but we have also seen that in some circumstances there will be statutory immunity from liability for the commission of certain torts.

The immunity is now contained in s219 of the Trade Union and Labour Relations (consolidation) Act 1992, which states:

"An act done by a person in contemplation or furtherance of a trade dispute is not actionable in tort on the ground only -

a) that it induces another person to break a contract or interferes or induces another person to interfere with its performance or

b) that it consists in his threatening that a contract (whether one to which he is a party or not) will be broken or its performance interfered with, or that he will induce another person to break a contract or interfere with its performance.

It will be seen therefore that protection is not afforded against the commission of any tort and that such torts as libel and slander, trespass, breach of statutory duty and so on have no immunity.

Trade dispute

The definition of a trade dispute is to be found in s 244(1) of the 1992 Act. This provides that the trade dispute is:

"a dispute between workers and their employer which relates wholly or mainly to....... terms and conditions of employment, or physical

81

conditions, engagement or non-engagement, or termination or suspension of employment, allocation of work, matters of discipline, membership or otherwise of a trade union, facilities for officials of trade unions and machinery for negotiation"

Trade union liability

The 1906 Trade Disputes Act introduced immunity from tortious liability for trade unions. This blanket immunity was removed by the Employment Act 1982 and now a union has the same immunity as its individual members. There is a statutory limit on the damages that can be awarded against a union, first introduced in 1982 and now contained in s22 of the 1992 Consolidation Act. The amount of damages depends on the number of members the trade union has. If there are less than 5,000 the maximum is £10,000. Between 5,000 and 25,000 the maximum is £50,000. Between 25,000 and 50,000 the maximum is £125,000 and over 100,000 the limit is £250,000. Each separate action may result in the maximum being imposed. Therefore, if more than one employer takes action against the union then the limit can be imposed separately for each employer. Furthermore, the limit only applies to damages and not for fines for contempt. Thus in the NGA dispute against the Stockport messenger in 1984 the union was fined £675,000 for contempt.

Loss of trade union immunity

Trade Union Immunity depends on the protected torts being committed and the balloting and notice requirements being complied with. Breach of any of these conditions will render the union liable for any tortious wrongs committed. A ballot is required in respect of any act done by a trade union, that is, in respect of any action authorised or endorsed by the union. Entitlement to vote must be accorded to all members of the union who will be induced to take part in the action and the ballot will be ineffective if this provision is not complied with.

Picketing

Picketing is a method by which a trade union can strengthen a strike. It can prevent workers from entering the workplace and so increase the disruption to the employer. The problem with picketing from a legal point of view is that it involves a consideration of both the civil and criminal law.

The criminal law becomes involved because the fact that picketing involves a group of people standing around can create criminal liability. In addition, pickets will normally interfere with contracts, be committing a trespass and often be committing a private nuisance, so rendering them potentially liable in tort. As such it is necessary to consider all the potential liability and look at the immunity.

Criminal liability, for example may be committing the offence of obstructing the highway, obstructing a police officer during the course of his duty or causing a public nuisance generally.

Civil liability might be that of committing a private nuisance, which is unlawful interference with an individuals enjoyment of his land, trespass to the highway or general economic torts such as breach of contract of employment.

Immunity for pickets is contained in s 220 of the 1992 Act. This renders it lawful for a person, in contemplation or furtherance of a trade dispute, to attend at or near his own place of work for the purpose of peacefully obtaining or communicating information, or peacefully persuading a person to work or not to work. In addition, a trade union official may peacefully picket at or near the place of work of a member of the union whom he is accompanying or whom he represents Unemployed employees are allowed to picket their former place of work if their employment was terminated in connection with the trade dispute or the dismissal gave rise to the trade dispute.

Remedies

Obviously, although the individual member commits the tort, it is more beneficial for an employer to sue the union, hence the removal of blanket union immunity in 1982. The majority of employers, however, do not want damages but rather want to prevent the action from commencing or to stop it as soon as possible. The most common remedy sought is that of injunctive relief. If the union fails to comply with an injunction the two methods of enforcement are committal for contempt and sequestration of the union assets. The court may imprison for contempt, fine or order security for good behaviour.

The 2002 Employment Act-Union Learning Representatives

The 2002 EA, S.43 provides for time off for Union learning Representatives. These provisions are similar to time off rights for Health and Safety Representatives. They allow time of for Union appointees, working in the interests of members of trade unions to:

- Analyse learning or training needs
- Provide information about or promote learning or training
- Arrange learning or training
- Consult with employers about any of the above

5

Discrimination in Employment

In this chapter a number of Acts of Parliament are considered. The earlier enactments have been subject to considerable amendment by subsequent legislation and it is important to refer to the amended rather than original legislation.

The enactment's which will be considered are the Equal Pay Act 1970, as amended by the Sex Discrimination Act 1975 and the Equal pay (amendment) regulations 1983, the Sex Discrimination Act 1975 (as amended by the Sex Discrimination Act 1986) and the Race Relations Act 1976. We will also look at the Disability Discrimination Act 1996.

Equal Pay

In broad terms, the Equal Pay Act 1970, as amended by the 2002 Employment Act, is concerned with less favourable treatment of one person relative to another in respect of matters governed by the contract under which a person is employed whereas the Sex Discrimination Act 1975 deals with less favourable treatment in matters not governed by the contract, on grounds of sex and/or marital status.

The Equal Pay Act 1970 has been influenced by the Treaty of Rome and the effect of certain European Community Directives have been considerable in this area and have significant practical consequences for any applicant contemplating bringing an action alleging breach of the 1970 Act.

Article 119 of the Treaty of Rome provides that: "each member state shall maintain the application of the principle that men and women should receive equal pay for equal work. For the purpose of this article, pay means the ordinary basic or minimum wage or salary and any other consideration, whether in cash or kind, which the worker receives, directly or indirectly in respect of his employment from his employer. The Article is directly enforceable by individuals in the courts of member states of the EEC.

The 2002 Employment Act introduces the right of the employee to give the employer a questionnaire in order to ascertain whether or not the employer is actually paying and treating equally. The employer does not have to comply. For further details go to chapter three, Remuneration.

Sex Discrimination Act 1975

In relation to employment, the Sex Discrimination Act is intended to render discrimination on the grounds of sex and/or the fact that a person is married, unlawful as regards those areas of employment not dealt with by the terms of the contract. The Act renders discrimination on the above grounds unlawful except in the following cases.

a) Discrimination by way of special treatment afforded to women in connection with pregnancy or childbirth.

b) Where in the previous year there were no or few members of one sex doing a particular job, discrimination in favour of members of that sex is allowed.

c) Discrimination in the selection, promotion or training of a person is permissible where being a man or woman is a genuine occupational qualification.

d) There are special rules relating to the police, prison officers and ministers of religion.

e) There are special rules relating to death or retirement. The position here has been much influenced by community law which in turn led to the amendment of the Sex Discrimination Act 1986. Under Community law it is quite clear that the domestic legislation of a member state may fix discriminatory retirement ages.

Section 6 of the Act provides that the following areas of employment are within the scope of the act.

a) Arrangements for selecting of employees and making offers of employment.

b) The terms upon which employment is offered but not the terms themselves when employment has been obtained, this latter matter being within the scope of the Equal Pay Act.

c) Access to promotion, training, transfer or any other benefit, facilities or services.

d) Dismissal or the subjecting of a person to any other detriment, e.g., suspension from work.

It is unlawful to publish, or cause to be published an advertisement which indicates, or might reasonably indicate, an intention to do an act which is contrary to the Act.

The meaning of discrimination. The Act embodies three kinds of discrimination, direct discrimination (unfavourable treatment on grounds of race, sex etc. Indirect discrimination-this is where the complainant must demonstrate that the employer applies a requirement or condition which he applies or would apply to members of the other sex/single persons. That it is to the complainants detriment because he or she cannot comply with it.

An example of the operation of this provision would be where an employer requires all his employees to be over six feet tall. This could only be justified if the employer could demonstrate that the job demanded it.

One important case in this area is Price v Civil Service Commission (1978) Held: a civil service condition that candidates for certain posts should be no more than 28 years of age was indirect discrimination because women in their late twenties were frequently occupied in having and rearing children.

Discrimination by victimisation. S4 deals with discrimination against a person who has brought proceedings, given evidence, information, alleged a contravention etc under the Sex Discrimination Act or Equal Pay Act. Such a person must not be treated less favourably by the alleged discriminator than another person in those circumstances was or would be treated.

In relation to discrimination on grounds of sex (as opposed to discrimination against married persons) s7 provides that certain kinds of employment are excluded from the operation of the Act, namely where being a member of one sex is a "genuine occupational qualification" for the job. Two general points should be noted:

 a) These provisions do not apply to the terms upon which employment is offered, dismissal or subjecting a person to any other detriment.

 b) These provisions do not apply to the filling of a vacancy where the employer already has male (or female) employees capable of filling it and whom it would be reasonable to employ on those duties and whose numbers are sufficient to meet the employers likely requirements without undue inconvenience.

Being a man or woman is a genuine occupational qualification for a job where the essential nature of the job calls for a man for reasons of physiology or authenticity e.g. actors, models etc. In addition where the job needs to be held by a man to preserve decency or privacy or the job is likely to involve the holder doing work or living in a private home and needs to be held by a same sex person because objections might be raised to a member of the opposite sex in attendance.

Also, the nature or the location of the establishment effectively requires the employee to live in and in the absence of separate sleeping accommodation and sanitary facilities, it is not reasonable to expect the employer to provide such things. In addition, the nature of the establishment where the work is done, i.e. a hospital or prison requires that the job be done by a man.

Race Relations Act 1976

The 1976 Act is concerned with discrimination on grounds of colour, race, nationality, or ethnic or national origin. Some difficulty has been experienced over the question of the meaning of ethnic origin and in particular its relationship with race. An important defining case in this respect was Mandla v Lee (1983). The House of Lords resolved the matter. The question was whether Sikhs are a group of persons defined by ethnic origin so as to fall within the protection of the Act. It was held that Sikhs did constitute an ethnic group. "Ethnic" was used in the Act in a sense much wider than that of "race" and an ethnic group can be identified by some or all of such essential factors as a long history, cultural tradition, common geographical origin, common language and a common religion. It should be noted that a racial group cannot be defined by the factor of language alone.

The 1976 Act is concerned not only with employment but covers also such things as the provision of services, housing etc.

There are a number of exceptions to the 1976 Act including where being of a certain race etc is deemed to be a genuine occupational qualification, such as specific providers of services to defined communities.

The Act may be enforced by individuals but the Commission for Racial Equality has wide powers. The Commission for Racial Equality is empowered to issue codes of practice on certain matters.

Discrimination on the grounds of disability

In 1995 the Disability Discrimination Act was passed. In relation to employment, it makes all employers of over 20 employees or more legally liable for discrimination against disabled people. Part 11 of the Act, relating to employment, came into force at the end of 1996 at which time there will be a code of practice in force to help on interpretation.

To be protected against discrimination an individual must be a person who has a disability or had a disability. Disability is defined as physical or mental impairment, which has a substantial and long-term effect on the person's ability to carry out day to day activities.

In relation to employment the individual is protected against discrimination. It should be noted that the Act only mentions discrimination on the grounds of disability and thus, unlike the Race Relations Act and Sex Discrimination Act will allow an employer to positively discriminate in the case of a person with a disability.

The Act, in s4, outlines acts of discrimination. These principally cover the arrangements for appointing employees, the terms on which employment is offered and refusal of employment. It is also unlawful to discriminate in the terms of employment, in the opportunities offered for training, promotion, transfer or any other benefit or to dismiss a person because of disability.

Section 11 provides for limited protection in relation to advertisements. Monitoring of the legislation will be by the National Disability Council.

6

Termination of Employment

There are a number of ways in which a contract of employment may come to an end. At common law, a contract of employment can be validly terminated by an employer giving notice to an employee in accordance with the terms of the contract or, in the absence of such a term, by giving reasonable notice. If sufficient notice was given, the employee had no further rights and this meant that dismissal could be entirely arbitrary. However, in recent times provisions have been introduced whereby an employee may be entitled to compensation for loss of job despite the fact that he was given notice.

It should be noted that once notice has been given, it can only effectively be withdrawn with the consent of the other party.

Dismissal with notice

The length of notice, which must be given by an employer to an employee, is determined by reference to the following criteria to be applied in the following order:

a) Express terms of the contract. if the contract of employment expressly provides for a period of notice, this must be observed unless that period is less than the statutory minimum to which that particular employee is entitled under d) below.

b) In the absence of an express term it may be impossible to imply a term into the contract, for example, by custom. Again, such a period may not be less than the statutory custom.

c) If there is no express or implied term of the contract, the courts may rely on a reasonable period. What is "reasonable" depends upon such factors as the status of the employee, salary, length of employment with that employer, age etc. The "reasonable" period cannot be less than the statutory minimum.

d) Statutory minimum. In the absence of any of the above criteria, or where they produce a period less than the following, the statutory minimum in s86 of the 1996 Act must be applied in respect of those employees covered by that section. Section 86 provides that for an employee continuously employed for between one month and two years, the notice period is one week; for an employee employed for more than two years, he is entitled to one week for each year of continuous employment subject to a maximum of twelve weeks notice after twelve years of employment.

These rights do not apply to a contract for the performance of a specific task, which is not expected to last for more than three months.

Summary dismissal

Summary dismissal is where an employer dismisses an employee without giving the employee the amount of notice to which that individual is entitled. If there is no justification, such dismissal is wrongful and an action can be brought.

The remedy for wrongful dismissal is damages representing the loss of wages during the period of notice that ought to have been given. In addition, wrongful dismissal may also be unfair dismissal within the meaning of the 1978 Act.

Circumstances which justify summary dismissal

The question of what justifies summary dismissal is not one that can be answered with a simple rule since each case must be decided according to the particular circumstances. However, a general principle has emerged that summary dismissal is justified if the conduct of the employee is such that it prevents further satisfactory continuance of the relationship. This was the finding in Sinclair v Neighbour. (1967)

The status of the employee in question is a relevant consideration as is the fact that the employee has a history of misconduct as opposed to an isolated incident.

Dismissals Procedure

If the contract states that dismissal is to be according to an established pattern (e.g. that there will be two warnings before dismissal occurs) it is a breach of contract if the procedure is not observed. (Tomlinson v L.M.S Rly (1944). If the contract states that the dismissal may only occur for certain specified reasons, a dismissal is wrongful if the reason for the dismissal is other than specified in the contract.

However, it should be noted that the 2002 Employment Act has introduced the obligation on an employer to include a statutory disciplinary and grievance procedure which must be in the contracts or written terms and must be followed before any dismissal proceedings can take place.

Waiver of rights

If an employee's conduct justified a summary dismissal, the right must have been exercised within a reasonable time of the conduct, which allegedly justified the action since delay may amount to a waiver of the breach of contract.

Employee leaving

An employee is entitled to terminate employment at any time by giving the amount of notice required by the contract. If the employee is deemed to have been entitled to terminate employment by reason of the employer's conduct that may constitute a constructive dismissal and the fact that he gave notice makes no difference. If an employer's attitude causes an employee to terminate his contract without notice, this may well constitute constructive dismissal and the employee may act accordingly.

Termination by agreement

The parties to a contract of employment as with any other contract, may terminate their relationship by agreement at any time upon such terms as they may agree, e.g. payment of money as a golden handshake. It should be noted that a termination by agreement is not a dismissal for the purposes of the redundancy and unfair dismissals provisions of the 1996 Act. However, the tribunals are concerned to ensure that any alleged agreement to terminate a contract of employment is real and not merely a result of pressure imposed on an employee who is unaware of the significance of agreeing to terminate the contract and who faces dismissal as an alternative to so agreeing.

Termination by frustration

Frustration occurs whenever the law recognises that without default of either party a contractual obligation has become incapable of being performed because the circumstance in which performance would be called for would render it a thing different from that which was undertaken by the contract. Lord Radcliffe in Davis Contractors v Fareham UDC (1956).

In the context of a contract of employment, the term frustration means that circumstances have arisen, without the fault of either party, that make it impossible for the contract to be performed in the way that may be reasonably expected and the contract automatically terminates without the need for notice to be given. Frustration of the contract is not deemed to be dismissal for legislative purposes.

Examples of frustration may be: sickness In Notcutt v Universal Equipment Co (1986), a worker with 27 years service, who was two years from retirement suffered a permanently incapacitating heart attack. The court decided that this rendered performance of the contract impossible and therefore the contract was frustrated as he was unable to perform his obligation to work. The employee was therefore not entitled to sick pay during his period of notice.

Imprisonment is another example, however this has caused problems. Recently, however, the Court of Appeal has allowed a four-year apprenticeship contract to be frustrated by a six months Borstal sentence: FC Shepherd LTD v Jerrom (1986). In this case court held that such a period of imprisonment made the performance of the contract impossible. As with the sickness, the courts will tend to look at each case on its own merits without applying hard and fast rules.

Action for wrongful dismissal

An employee who has been wrongfully dismissed may bring an action for damages against his former employer representing the amount of wages owed to him in respect of work already done and in respect of wages that the employee would have earned had he been given the amount of notice to which he was entitled. The amount of wages lost is determined by the ordinary principles of common law and includes all sums connected with the job, such as loss of tips etc.

Damages for wrongful dismissal cannot normally include compensation for injured feelings or pride or the fact that future earnings may be affected. The object of damages is to compensate the injured party for what he actually lost, not to punish the party in breach of contract, and therefore the courts have developed principles to ensure that the employee who has been wrongfully dismissed receives compensation only for his actual loss.

Damages against employee

Where an employee fails to give sufficient notice to his employer, the employer may sue the employee for damages representing the loss, which follows from the breach of contract. In practice, such actions are infrequent because the loss is often minimal.

Specific performance

Specific performance is an order from the court directing that the parties to a contract perform their contractual obligations. It is a fundamental principle of labour law that specific performance is never granted to compel performance of a contract of employment and this principle is now embodied in s 235 of the Trade Union and Labour Relations (Consolidation) Act 1992.

Injunction

An injunction is an order from a court forbidding certain conduct, e.g. the breaking of a term of the contract of employment. Hence it may be used to prevent a breach of a covenant restraining an employee from taking employment with a rival of his former employer. The courts usually refuse to grant an injunction if it compels performance.

By virtue of the Trade Union and Labour Relations Act 1992, no court may issue an injunction if the effect of such an order would be to compel an employee to do any work or to attend any place to work.

However, where the injunction compelling performance is to the benefit of the employee, the court may be prepared to grant such an order. In Hill v CA Parsons LTD (1972) the defendant employers wished to enter into an agreement with an organisation of workers whereby it was agreed that all employers in certain sections, including the plaintiff, would be obliged to join that organisation. This arrangement was legal at the time but under the Industrial Relations Act 1971 it would have been invalid. The plaintiff did not wish to join the organisation and he was dismissed with four weeks notice. The Court of Appeal held that he was wrongfully dismissed since he was entitled to at least six months notice and furthermore an injunction was awarded which prevented the employee from being dismissed until that time elapsed by which time he would have a remedy under the 1971 Act.

Declaration

A declaration is an order from the court, which simply determines the rights of the parties in the case. It has no binding force in itself and is not available to all employees being restricted to those persons whose employment is derived from statute.

Written statement of reasons for dismissal

An employee who has been continuously employed for at least two years and who has been dismissed, subject to the statutory provisions of the 2002 Act and the following of a formal procedure, is entitled to receive, upon request, a written statement of the reasons for his dismissal.

A claim may be presented to an industrial tribunal by an employee that his employer has "unreasonably" refused to provide a written statement of the reasons for dismissal or that it is inadequate or untrue. The right to a written statement only arises where the employee has been dismissed by his employer.

Suspension

In accordance with the general principle that an employer fulfils his contractual obligations by paying wages in accordance with the contract of employment, he may suspend an employee on full wages without breach of contract. An employer may only suspend an employee without pay if the contract expressly or impliedly provided for this. If the contract does not so provide, it is a breach of contract. Therefore, an employee who is suspended without contractual authority may treat himself as dismissed and claim accordingly.

7

Unfair Dismissal

The present law relating to unfair dismissal is to be found in the Employment Rights Act 1996.

The significance of the concept of unfair dismissal is that it represents a further, and most important, step towards recognising the property right, which an employee has in his job. Additionally, it is no longer possible for an employer to end a contract by simply giving notice and thereby totally discharging his responsibilities. The threat of dismissal is no longer quite so important since the employee has a remedy if the threat is implemented.

The 1996 Act provides that, subject to certain specified exceptions, every employee has the right not to be unfairly dismissed. It should be noted that a complaint of unfair dismissal does not depend upon the employer having acted in breach of contract but simply that the employer has terminated the contract in circumstances which are unfair.

Certain categories of employees are excluded: employees who, at the effective date of termination of the contract have been continuously employed for less than one year, (1999 Employment Rights Act, came into force June 1999) persons over retiring age, persons employed in the police service, share fishermen, employees who ordinarily work outside Great Britain, employees employed on fixed term contracts and persons covered by a designated dismissals procedure agreement.

Dismissal

If an action for unfair dismissal is to succeed, the employee must first establish that he was dismissed within the meaning of the Act. The employee must establish constructive dismissal if alleged. The Act provides that:

"an employee shall be treated as dismissed by his employer if the contract under which he is employed by the employer is terminated by the employer whether it is so terminated by notice or without notice or where under that contract he is employed for a fixed term, that term expires without being renewed under the same contract or the employee terminates that contract, with or without notice, in circumstances such that he is entitled to terminate it without notice by reason of the employers conduct".

The Act refers to the concept of so-called "constructive; dismissal. If an employee leaves employment entirely voluntarily, there is no dismissal but if he leaves because of the employers conduct then it may be deemed "constructive"

The courts and tribunals have been concerned to define the circumstances in which an employee is entitled to regard himself as having been constructively dismissed. In Western Excavating LTD v Sharp (1978) the tribunals found that sufficiently unreasonable behaviour on the part of the employer entitled an employee to leave his job and claim constructive dismissal. However, the Court of Appeal rejected the unreasonableness test and established that the correct test is one based on strict contractual principles. Accordingly, an employee is only able successfully to argue constructive dismissal where the employer has breached the contract in such a way as to justify the employee in treating himself as discharged from further performance. The action of an employer may involve breach of an express or implied term.

When is dismissal unfair?

The expression "unfair dismissal" is in no sense a commonsense expression capable of being understood by the person in the street. Whether a dismissal is unfair is affected, but not conclusively determined, by whether one or both parties has broken the terms of the contract of employment. The employer cannot, in seeking to show that a dismissal was not unfair rely on alleged misconduct not known to him at the time of the dismissal. An otherwise fair dismissal is not automatically rendered unfair by a failure to give proper notice.

Reasonableness. It is for the employer to establish the reason for the dismissal. The tribunal must then satisfy itself as to whether the employer acted reasonably or unreasonably. The EAT laid down the following general principles in Iceland Frozen Foods v Jones (1982):

a) In applying the provisions of the 1996 Act a tribunal must consider the reasonableness of the employers conduct and not simply whether they (the members of the tribunal) consider the dismissal unfair.

b) In judging the reasonableness of the employer's conduct a tribunal must not substitute its own decision as to what was the right course to adopt for that of the employer.

c) In many cases there is a band of reasonable responses to the employees conduct within which one employer might take one view and another quite reasonably another.

d) The function of the tribunal is to determine whether in the particular circumstances the decision to dismiss fell within the band of reasonable responses, which a reasonable employer might have adopted. If the dismissal falls within the band it is fair. If it falls outside the band it is unfair.

In deciding whether an employer acted reasonably, the industrial tribunal is required to have regard to the provisions of the ACAS Code of Practice; Disciplinary Code of Practice and Procedures in Employment. In broad terms, this provides that the disciplinary rules and procedures ought to have been made known to each employee and that a disciplinary procedure ought to contain certain essential procedures.

Reasons for dismissal

There are five categories of reasons, which, if one is established by the employer, may make the dismissal fair provided that the tribunal is satisfied that the employer acted reasonably. These are as follows:

a) Capability or qualification

b) Conduct

c) Redundancy

d) Illegality of continued employment

e) Some other substantial reason.

In addition, an employer in certain circumstances, can dismiss an employee for reasons connected to pregnancy. Usually, it is automatically unfair to do so unless the employer can establish that at the effective date of termination, because of her pregnancy, she:

a) is or will have become incapable of adequately doing the work she is employed to do or: or

b) cannot or will not be able to do the work she is employed to do without a contravention (either by her or her employer) of a duty or restriction imposed by law.

In Brown v Stockton on Tees Borough Council (1988) the House of Lords held that if a woman was selected for redundancy because she is pregnant, such a dismissal is automatically unfair. Indeed, Lord Griffith stated that "it surely cannot have been intended that an employer should be entitled to take advantage of a redundancy situation to weed out his pregnant employer". However, even where the circumstances of a and b above apply, the dismissal is still unfair if the employer has a suitable vacancy, i.e. appropriate for a pregnant woman to do and not substantially less favourable than her existing employment in relation to the nature, terms and place of employment, which he fails to offer her.

Dismissal for trade union reasons

References in this section are to the Trade Union and Labour Relations (Consolidation) Act 1992.

Trade Union membership or activities. Except in exceptional cases, a dismissal is automatically unfair if the employee can establish that the principal reason for it was that the employer was, or proposed to become, a member of an independent trade union, or that the employee had taken or proposed to take part in the activities of an independent trade union at any appropriate time or that the employee was not a member of any or a particular trade union, or had refused or proposed to refuse to become or remain a member.

Other reasons for dismissal

An industrial tribunal cannot determine whether a dismissal was fair or unfair if it is known that at the date of dismissal the employer was conducting or instituting a lock out or the complainant was taking part in a strike or other industrial action, unless it is shown:

a) that one or more relevant employees of the same employer have not been dismissed: or

b) that any such employee has, before the expiry of the period of three months beginning with the employee's date of dismissal, been offered re-engagement and that the complainant has not been offered re-engagement.

National security

If an employee has shown to have been dismissed on grounds of national security, as evidenced by a certificate signed by or on behalf of a minister of the Crown, the tribunal must dismiss the complaint. In Council of Civil Service Unions v Minister for the Civil Service (1985) (the GCHQ case), the court held that the requirements of national security outweighed those of fairness when the minister decided to ban trade unions at GCHQ, without consultation with the trade unions. Workers who refused to give up their trade union membership were subsequently fairly dismissed.

Procedure

An employee who considers that he has been unfairly dismissed may present a complaint to the Central Office of Industrial Tribunals within three months of the effective date of termination or within such further period as the tribunal considers reasonable in a case where it is satisfied that it was not reasonably practicable for the complaint to be presented within a time period of three months.

Where the dismissal is unfair (failure to offer re-engagement where the dismissal is connected with a lockout or strike) the time limit is six months from the date of dismissal. A copy of the application is sent to the employer as respondent. If the employer wishes to contest any aspect of the complaint, he must enter a "notice of appearance" within 14 days, although tribunals have a wide discretion to grant an extension of time. Once this has happened, a date is set down for the hearing of the case by an industrial tribunal.

Conciliation

A copy of the application is also sent to a conciliation officer. He is under a statutory duty, either at the request of the parties or on his own initiative, to endeavor to promote a voluntary settlement of the issue, either by way of an agreement to reinstate or re-engage the complainant or an agreement as to the payment of compensation in respect of the dismissal. There is no legal duty upon the parties to co-operate with the conciliation officer.

Pre-hearing Assessments

Under the Industrial Tribunals Regulations (S! 1985/16) provision is made for a pre-hearing assessment of the case to be made at the request of either of the parties or on the notion of the tribunal itself. At the tribunal, it is for the complainant to establish that he was dismissed (unless dismissal is conceded). It is then for the tribunal to satisfy itself as to whether the dismissal was fair or unfair in accordance with the principles stated above.

If the dismissal is found to be unfair, the tribunal will consider the remedies, which may be awarded. An appeal, on a point of law only, lies from an Industrial Tribunal to the Employment Appeal Tribunal.

Remedies

Reinstatement and re-engagement orders. If the tribunal finds the dismissal unfair, it must explain to the complainant the remedies available and ask if he wishes to be reinstated or re-engaged. If the employee indicates that this is his wish then the tribunal must consider whether it is practicable for the employer to comply with such an order. If the employer complies, but not fully, with a reinstatement or re-engagement order then, unless the tribunal is satisfied that it was not practicable to comply with the order, an additional award of compensation must be made.

If a reinstatement or re-engagement order is made but not complied with at all or if no such order is made, the tribunal must make an award of compensation on the basis of the following:

a) basic award, amount of which is calculated in line with redundancy payments;

b) compensatory award, being an amount that the tribunal considers just and equitable in all the circumstances having regard to the loss suffered by the complainant in consequence of the dismissal in so far as the loss is attributable to action taken by the employer subject to a maximum limit.

8

Redundancy

Compensation for redundancy was one of the first employment protection rights introduced into our law. The first piece if legislation was the Redundancy Payments Act 1965 and the law is now contained in the main in the Employment Rights Act 1996. In order to claim a redundancy payment an employee must have two years continuous service and be dismissed for reasons of redundancy. The definition of dismissal for redundancy purposes is contained within s 136 of the Employment Rights Act 1996.

These situations are the same as unfair dismissal: employer termination with or without notice, a fixed term contract expiring and constructive dismissal In addition, by s 139(4), if the employment is terminated by the death, dissolution or liquidation of the employer, or the appointment of a receiver, there is dismissal for reasons of redundancy.

The definition of redundancy is found in s 139(1) of the Act. This states that a redundancy has occurred if the dismissal is wholly or mainly attributable to:

a) the fact that his employer has ceased or intends to cease, to carry on the business for the purposes for which the employee was employed by him, or has ceased, or intends to cease, to carry on that business in the place where the employee was so employed or...

b) the fact that the requirements of that business for employees to carry out work of a particular kind, or for employees to carry out work of a particular kind in the place where he was so employed, have ceased or diminished or are expected to cease or diminish.

This means that the redundancy occurs in three situations - the employer increasing business, the employee moving his place of business or the employer reducing his labour force.

Misconduct and redundancy

Section 140(1) of the Employment Rights Act 1996 provides that in certain situations the employee will be disentitled to a redundancy payment. This occurs when the employee terminates the contract where:

a) the employee commits an act of misconduct and the employer dismisses without notice or

b) the employee commits an act of misconduct and the employer dismisses with shorter notice than the redundancy notice or

c) the employer, when the redundancy notice expires, gives the employee a statement in writing that the employer is entitled, by virtue of the employee's conduct, to dismiss without notice.

There are two exceptions to this. By s140 (2) where an employee, while under notice of redundancy, takes part in a strike or other industrial action to protest against the redundancies. If however, an employee who is on strike is selected for redundancy, the tribunal will have no jurisdiction to hear the case unless there are selective dismissals (Simmons v Hoover (1977)).

By S 143 the employer can extend the redundancy notice period and require the employees to work in order to make up the days lost by the industrial action and if the employees lose they disentitle themselves to a redundancy payment.

Suitable alternative employment

If the employer offers the employee his old job back or a different job which is suitable alternative employment, the new contact starts on the termination of the old or within four weeks of the old contract expiring and the employee unreasonably refuses the offer he is disentitled to a redundancy payment by virtue of sections 141(2) and (3). The section therefore means that two questions must be asked: is the offer suitable alternative employment and is the employee's refusal of that offer reasonable.

Trial period in new employment

If the terms of the new contract differ (wholly or in part) from the old contract, then by s138 the employee is entitled to a trial period. By subsection (3) the statutory trial period is four weeks, but this can be extended by the employees contract as long as the period is in writing and specified precisely. If the employee is dismissed during the trial period, he is treated as being dismissed for the reason his original contract ended, that is, redundancy, and on the date his original contract ended, so entitling him to claim a redundancy payment. If the employee resigns, he is treated as dismissed for redundancy, unless his resignation was unreasonable.

Lay off and short time working

In order to prevent redundancies, the employer may temporarily lay off his workers to put them on short time. By s147 a lay off is where no work or pay is provided by the employer. Short time working is where less than half a weeks pay is earned. By s148 where the lay off or short time has lasted for more than four consecutive weeks or six weeks in any thirteen, the employee can give notice to his employer that he intends to claim a redundancy payment. He must give the notice in writing. The employer has a defence if he can show that he reasonably expects to provide full time work for the next thirteen weeks and he raises this defence in written counter notice served within seven days of receipt of the employees intention to claim.

Redundancy compensation

A redundancy payment is calculated in the same way as the basic award for unfair dismissal and is therefore based on age and years of service. However, unlike the basic award, periods of employment below the age of 18 do not count and the employee's period of continuity is deemed to start at his 18th birthday. (Employment Rights Act 1996 s 211(2). Again, unlike the basic award there is no deduction for contributory conduct, but like the basic award, there will be no reduction for each month the employee works in the year before he attains the normal retirement age for the job, so that on reaching the age, or 65, whichever is lower, entitlement to a redundancy payment ceases.

If the redundancy is caused by the employer's insolvency, the employee may make a claim for a redundancy payment to the Department of Employment under s166 of the Employment Rights Act 1996. While the Employee ranks as a preferential creditor in his employer's insolvency, this will not be much use if the employer has no assets and therefore additionally the Department can pay certain sums to the employee from the National Insurance Fund. This can be up to eight weeks wages, up to six weeks holiday pay, a basic award and other payments.

Consultation

Failure to consult the employee about his redundancy may render the dismissal unfair. Unions must be consulted too. Where the employer has broken his statutory duty to consult, the union or employee representatives can apply to a tribunal for a protective award which is payable to those employees in respect of whom the representatives should have been consulted. Similar provisions relate to consultation where there is a transfer of an undertaking under the Transfer of Undertakings Regulations 1981. Where such a transfer takes place, Regulation 10 creates a duty on both the transferor and the transferee to inform the representatives.

The remedy for failure to comply with the consultation provisions under the regulations is found in Regulation 11. The employer can raise the defence of special circumstances. The maximum award which can be made under the Regulations is four weeks pay. This is set off against any protective award given to the employee. Since 1993, the duty on the tribunal to offset this payment against wages or payment in lieu of notice is removed.

9

Health and Safety

The Health and Safety at Work Act 1974.

Although not seen as implied duties in the contract of employment, it would be incomplete to talk about the employer's liability in relation to the safety of his employees without a brief overview of the statutory provisions.

The 1974 Act was introduced as a result of the Robens Committee report of 1972. The Committee found that the law on health and safety was piecemeal and badly structured, with eleven pieces of major legislation supplemented by over 500 supplementary statutory provisions. The majority of the law based liability on occupation of premises. The Committee proposed a unification of the law, basing liability on employment not occupation of premises.

The Committees findings were embodied in the Health and Safety at work Act 1974. The aim of the Act is twofold - to lay down general duties across the whole area of employment, and to provide a unified system of enforcement under the control of the Health and Safety Executive and local authorities. General duties are imposed upon various types of people, for example employers, suppliers and manufacturers, with the aim of ensuring a safe working environment.

Section 2(1) lays down the general duty on employers: it "It shall be the duty of every employer to ensure, so far as is reasonably practicable, the health, safety and welfare of all his employees. This is further specified by subsection (2). The phrase to which all these duties are subject is "so far as is reasonably practicable". The basis of the duties under s 2(2) is that of employment - it covers duties owed by an employer to his employees; the duties, however, extend beyond the employment relationship. Section 3(1) provides that employers should conduct their business in such a way, "in so far as is reasonably practicable to protect persons other than their own employees from risks to their health and safety.

Liability is imposed not only on those who physically occupy premises but also on those who are responsible for the maintenance of such premises, or the access to and exit from the premises. In addition, liability is imposed against those responsible for safety and absence of risk concerning plant or substances used on the premises.

Protection of those other than employees is continued in s5. This imposes a duty on those who control work premises to use the best means practicable to prevent the emission of offensive or noxious substances and to render harmless any such substances, which are so emitted. This general duty overlaps with the more specific duties laid down in the Control of Pollution Act 1974.

The Act attempts to increase protection by imposing duties on designers, manufacturers, importers and suppliers. A chain of responsibility is therefore imposed from the design and manufacture of an article to its installation, use and maintenance. It can be seen, however, that the duties under the Act overlap and this demonstrates the stated aim of the legislation of accident prevention.

The duty owed to employees by s2 of the Act, if the Employer employs five or more persons he should have a general policy on health and safety and bring this policy to the notice of his employees. The policy should identify who is responsible for health and safety and should point out particular health and safety problems and arrangements for dealing with them. The policy should also cover such matters as training and supervision, inspection procedures, safety precautions and consultative arrangements. In addition, it must tell the employee how he can complain about any health and safety risk to which he feels he is being exposed. While the common law imposes no duty on the employee to look after his own health and safety, failure to do so could mean that any damages could be wiped out by the employer raising the defence of contributory negligence. given that the aim of the statutory duty is not to provide compensation, the Act places a duty on the individual employee to have regard to his own safety and that of those around him. Often, employers will make breach of health and safety regulations a disciplinary offence and in some case it may be fair to dismiss an employee for such a breach. In Rogers v Wicks and Wilson COIT 90/97 willful breach of a no smoking policy imposed for safety reasons was held to be a justifiable reason for dismissal.

Appendix 1
European legislation and UK compliance

The following is a list of the subject matter of the main European Directives concerning Employment law and how the UK government has responded and implemented them (or otherwise).

1. Safeguarding employees rights in transfers of undertakings (Acquired Rights Directive)

UK-Transfer of Undertakings Regulations (Protection of Employment 1981)

2. Protection of employees in the event of their employees insolvency

UK-Employment Rights Act 1996-Pensions Schemes Act 193.

3. Organisation of Working Time

UK-Working Time Regulations 1996

4. Protection of Young people at Work

UK-Working Time Regulations 1998-Working Time (Amendment(Regulations 2002

5. Posting of Workers

UK-Employment Relations Act 199-Equal Opportunities (Employment Legislation (Territorial Limits) Regulations 1999

6. Extending to the UK the Directive on the establishment of a European Works Council or a procedure for informing and consulting employees

UK-Transnational information and consultation of Employees Regulations 1999.

7. Extending to the UK the Directive on parental leave.

UK-Maternity and Parental Leave Regulations 1999.

8. Part time work

UK-Part-time workers (Prevention of less favourable Treatment) Regulations 2000

9. Fixed-term work

UK Fixed Term Employees (Prevention of less favourable treatment) Regulations 2002.

10. Summer time arrangements

UK-Summer time Act 1972.

There are a number of other directives that the UK has not complied with. However, the most important and significant areas have been complied with. For further information on directives you should go to the DTI website.

INDEX